THE FINANCIAL GUIDELINES
TAKING THE RIGHT STEP

THE FINANCIAL GUIDELINES
(How to start a Business)
Set-Up, Managing, Succession.

Table *of* Contents

Dedication

This book is dedicated to my father, Cinelas Franck Bonhomme, who played an integral role in shaping my business mindset. He was not only a provider but a devoted father who made sure to prioritize our relationship. His presence in my life was both productive and protective, always looking out for my well-being. He possessed a generous spirit and would give to others without hesitation. His life serves as a testament to the importance of resilience in every endeavor. Dad, I deeply regret not expressing how much I loved you while you were still here with us.

HOW TO START A BUSINESS

SET-UP, MANAGING, SUCCESSION

The Financial Guidelines in How to Start a Business-Set-Up, Managing, Succession

CONTACT US

FRANK BONHOMME
TEL: 901-657-5913
FAX: 888-758-9639
Www.thefinancialguidelines.com
Info@thefinancialguidelines.com
Address: 237-33 Jamaica Avenue
Bellerose, NY 11426

Editor: Luke Lurevs

INTRODUCTION

As well as being a business guide, this is a book about reflection; a book about mistakes made, successes secured, and lessons learned. It makes sense, then, that we begin these reflections by going back to my earliest days. In hindsight, even then I can recognize the passion for business that whirred inside of me. Growing up in a family of entrepreneurs, my father being a prominent figure in the Haitian business landscape, my exposure to the dynamic world of commerce began early in my life. His ownership of multiple properties and businesses exemplified the entrepreneurial spirit that ran through our family, a spirit that has been drilled into me and one that I hope to pass onto you, dear reader, through this book. Indeed, my mother actively managed some of the convenience stores owned by my father, and I vividly remember her taking trips from Haiti to Florida, where she would meticulously select merchandise to bring back and sell in her boutique. However, our relocation to the United States in 1986, a move prompted by political unrest and turmoil, forced my resilient parents to start anew. Despite facing language barriers and an almost-total unfamiliarity with the American workforce, they courageously embraced the challenge and began their journey in a foreign land. After all, a true business spirit transcends borders.

So, my business journey began aged 15, when I embarked on a paper route, fueled by my admiration for Wally, the suburban boy in the TV series *Leave It to Beaver*, who effortlessly delivered newspapers on his bicycle. Although the financial rewards were not substantial, the sense of accomplishment was immeasurable. Motivated by this, my teenage years saw me explore a plethora of entrepreneurial ventures and side hustles; I honed my skills in building and repairing computers, expertly installed radio systems in automobiles, and even pursued my passion as a Christian disk jockey. As I matured, so did my entrepreneurial ventures. In my twenties, I immersed myself in the world of self-employment, and proudly ran my own successful business.

Getting started officially in business involves several crucial steps, such as registering your business with the appropriate state and federal authorities, obtaining a tax identification number, and fulfilling all the necessary legal obligations set out by your local municipality. In the subsequent chapters, we will delve into the startup process in greater detail. Here, however, it might be worthwhile to condense my own business journey into a few short sentences. My operations began with extensive market research, conducted to assess the overall demand for my services. After all, no demands mean no sales! Efficiency played a pivotal role during the early stages of my business, and I rented a desk in the real estate office in which I worked as an agent. This arrangement allowed me to work on my business while waiting for potential buyers and renters. Thankfully, my realtor understood the situation since I was not earning hourly wages as one of their salespeople. This set-up came with another benefit, too: the ability to multitask. As my business gradually began to flourish, I relocated to a more prominent space. Still, it is vital to point out that such progression did not arise by luck or chance (or indeed with any great speed). It required tremendous effort, hard work, and a fair share of trial and error. I relentlessly promoted my business by distributing flyers day and night, seizing every opportunity to raise awareness (remember, demand is essential). Attending numerous networking events allowed me to forge valuable connections and cultivate relationships that have stood the test of time. Yet there were instances where it became necessary to part ways with certain clients. Yes, you heard it right – some individuals were simply not worth the hassle. In fact, I have dedicated a sub-chapter specifically to customer relationships, delving into the nuances of maintaining positive interactions with clients.

Throughout this book, I will candidly share the mistakes and successes that came to define this decades-long journey, hoping that you can learn from them and avoid the pitfalls I myself encountered. Perhaps above all, my objective over the following 160 pages is to illuminate the true *essence* of being a businessperson. In recent times, terms like "Boss Chick" and "Boss Man" have been popularized through music and social media platforms, embodying an apparently overwhelming desire for individuals to become their own bosses without fully comprehending the true demands and responsibilities that come with such a position. While I personally wish that everyone could experience the joys of entrepreneurship at least once in their lifetimes, I understand that not everyone understands the essential qualities required to be a successful boss. Many fail to realize that being a boss necessitates far greater dedication and effort than being an employee. As a business owner, for instance, I distinctly recall moments when I lacked motivation and was left trying to push myself to continue working. During my time as an employee, by contrast, I would simply take sick leave if I felt unwell or dejected. Moreover, every financial challenge that your business faces is one that impacts you personally, both from a monetary and mental perspective. Obtaining loans can prove arduous, particularly for minority or new businesses and especially during the initial stages where capital is crucial. During the infancy of a business, one must invest countless hours in building a solid client base and establishing foolproof systems that minimize errors. It is hard work, but the purpose of this book is not to deter your entrepreneurial attempts. Far from it, I want to show that, despite the heightened demands of running your own business, the rewards can be profoundly gratifying if approached with the right mindset, preparation and motivation.

Together, we will delve into the question of what *really* defines being a boss, and we will explore the industry-specific terminology associated with entrepreneurship. After examining the roles and responsibilities that accompany business ownership, we will evaluate whether you possess the necessary patience and customer service skills, or if hiring individuals with a business mindset would be a more suitable route to your success. We will discuss the importance of offering something unique to the market and understanding whether there is a genuine demand for your services. Equally as importantly, we will acknowledge that not everyone is cut out to actively run a business; passive investment can also provide opportunities for ownership. With our outline complete, let us begin.

CHAPTER ONE

ENTREPRENEURIAL EDUCATION AND CARRIER OUTLOOK

Today, the desire to become an entrepreneur is prevalent among individuals from various backgrounds and age groups. But what exactly does it mean to be an entrepreneur? Before you decide whether you really do aspire to be the "Boss Chick" or "Boss Man" heralded by the younger generations, let us discuss what such a position involves.

An entrepreneur can be described as somebody who undertakes the task of building and operating their own business. What sets them apart is their ownership stake in the venture, which grants them the potential to reap substantial profits should their endeavors prove successful. However, along with the prospects of financial gain, entrepreneurs also shoulder a significant amount of risk—a far greater burden compared to that of a regular employee within an established company. This entrepreneurial risk can manifest in various forms, such as the possibility of losing one's initial investment made or experiencing profound emotional distress, shame or embarrassment in the event of business failure.

Given the high stakes involved in starting and nurturing a prosperous business, it should come as no surprise that entrepreneurs typically share a specific set of skills that increase their chances of success. While some fortunate individuals seem to possess these skills innately, or at least cultivate them very early on, it is worth noting that others must acquire them through dedicated learning and experience. Ultimately, however, nobody is born a ready-made entrepreneur; Boss Baby exists only in the movies. Rather, the path to entrepreneurship always encompasses a blend of inherent abilities and the acquisition of knowledge and competencies that contribute to the growth and sustainability of your business.
One television show that captivates me is Shark Tank, a favorite among my family members. In the evenings, we gather around the living room, eagerly

watching as aspiring entrepreneurs present their innovative ideas to the esteemed *Sharks*[1]. We find great pleasure in witnessing the introduction of various concepts and the potential partnerships that may arise, and we like to place ourselves in the shoes of the potential investors.

During the show, one phrase frequently uttered by the Sharks resonates with us: "You have a business, but not an *investable* business." It highlights the distinction between having a promising idea and having a viable business model that can worthily attract investment. The Sharks often inquire about whether the entrepreneurs have patented their products, recognizing the importance of intellectual property protection, or whether the entrepreneur can prove that there exists a sizable market for their offerings.

Additionally, the Sharks carefully assess the character and potential of each aspiring business partner. Some entrepreneurs specifically seek out Damon John, an expert in the garment industry, as their ideal partner. This reminds me of how the Rockefeller family, led by John D. Rockefeller, had a dedicated team to manage their wealth. Similarly, each Shark has a team of professionals behind the scenes who help run their venture capital businesses. Delving deeper into the world of venture capital, we will explore the concept further in the subsequent sub-chapter. First, however, let us return to our goal of identifying the skills that are most prevalent among the entrepreneurial community.

UNDERSTANDING ENTREPRENEURIAL SKILLS

Entrepreneurs play a vital and transformative role in any economy, utilizing their skills and initiative to foresee emerging needs and introduce innovative ideas to the market. The realm of entrepreneurship presents tantalizing rewards to those who bravely navigate the risks inherent in establishing a startup, including the potential for financial prosperity, recognition, and

---

[1] For those who are not familiar with it, Shark Tank (or Dragon's Den in the UK) is a show in which entrepreneurs deliver business presentations in search of investment from a panel of esteemed venture capitalists (or *sharks*).

ongoing growth prospects. Conversely, the journey of entrepreneurship is not without its perils, as failures can result in substantial losses and diminished prominence within the competitive market landscape.

The allure of charting one's own path, assuming the role of ultimate decision-maker and reaping substantial financial gains has long captivated the imaginations of aspiring entrepreneurs. However, a vast array of potential challenges accompanies this pursuit. Guarantees of steady income dissipate, the comforting umbrella of employer-sponsored benefits fades away, and in the unfortunate event of business losses, personal assets may be at risk, transcending the boundaries of a corporation's balance sheet. However, there exist established principles that can help reduce these risks, acting as guiding lights throughout the entrepreneurial voyage. The traits outlined below encompass the fundamental attributes necessary to flourish as a prosperous entrepreneur.

1. **Communication**

In the realm of entrepreneurship, effective communication stands as a non-negotiable attribute for every individual. Whether operating as a 'solopreneur' or steering a multinational conglomerate, it is paramount to possess a deep understanding of how to convey information, ideas, and vision in a compelling and impactful manner.

An entrepreneur's ability to communicate extends far and wide, encompassing various facets of their journey in business. From engaging with employees and investors to captivating new customers, creditors, peers, and mentors, the skill to effectively articulate the value proposition of one's company becomes a determining factor in its success or failure. Furthermore, a truly adept entrepreneur must navigate and master a diverse array of communication channels and mediums. This includes excelling in one-on-one and face-to-face conversations (consider the famous 'elevator pitch'), adeptly steering group discussions, crafting persuasive written communications, and skillfully harnessing the power of email, webpages, directory listings and social media profiles to convey their message with precision and impact. Only through the mastery of these various forms of communication can an entrepreneur foster lasting connections, inspire trust, and drive the growth and prosperity of their venture.

2. Sales

The art of sales intertwines seamlessly with the essential communication skills required for entrepreneurial success. As an entrepreneur, one must possess an ability to sell with finesse, persuading and influencing others to embrace their vision and offerings. This encompasses a multifaceted selling approach whereby the entrepreneur must skillfully pitch their business ideas to potential investors, compellingly promote their products or services to customers, and authentically present themselves to attract and retain talented employees. Of course, effective communication lies at the heart of such endeavors.

In the early stages of a venture, it is only natural for entrepreneurs to assume the role of the primary salesperson within their companies. These initial sales experiences serve as a crucible for developing and honing the skills needed to demonstrate value and generate enthusiasm among all stakeholders, both internal and external to the organization. Proficiency in sales extends beyond mere deal closures, encompassing the establishment of lasting connections, the promotion of customer satisfaction, and the cultivation of a robust sense of purpose and dedication among team members. Ultimately, the art of sales serves as a cornerstone for any entrepreneur's journey, laying the groundwork for the long-term success and sustainability of their business.

3. Focus

Embarking on the journey of entrepreneurship is akin to traversing a tumultuous hiking trail decorated with both exhilarating triumphs and disheartening setbacks. During this journey, another pivotal trait that sets accomplished entrepreneurs apart is their capacity to sustain concentration and perseverance in the face of challenges.

Emotional instability stands as one of the primary risks facing entrepreneurs on their arduous voyage. The inherent uncertainties, challenges, and unexpected hurdles that pepper the entrepreneurial landscape can take a toll on an individual's emotional wellbeing and—if the business owner is not prepared to battle these—your start-up can quickly fail. Imagine a car with an incapacitated driver; it would not stay on the road for long. A resilient and accomplished entrepreneur, on the other hand, possesses the capacity to remain composed and composed, steadfastly weathering the storms that arise and steering their business toward clearer roads. They cultivate the skill of focusing on the bigger picture, anchoring their thoughts and actions with an end goal in mind.

The importance of focus transcends the ability to concentrate and work toward your goals, then. It encompasses a resilient mindset that perseveres in the face of challenges. It is through this unwavering dedication and clarity of purpose that successful entrepreneurs navigate the unpredictable terrain of entrepreneurship. By remaining resolute, they forge ahead, demonstrating their mettle, and ultimately emerging victorious, having translated their aspirations into tangible reality.

4. Ability to Learn

In life and business alike, the ability to learn stands as a paramount skill. Entrepreneurship is an unpredictable path where unforeseen challenges and setbacks are bound to arise. In order to navigate these inevitable fluctuations, entrepreneurs require a steadfast commitment to continuous learning, coupled with an insatiable desire to expand their knowledge.

A high capacity to learn is a prerequisite for entrepreneurial triumph. Those who possess this skill approach every situation as an opportunity for growth, embracing both successes and failures as valuable sources of insight. Embracing failure as a learning experience becomes a catalyst for personal and professional development. By analyzing the factors that contributed to setbacks, entrepreneurs gain a deeper understanding of the intricacies of business and acquire the wisdom necessary to make better-informed decisions moving forward. Indeed, many of the most important lessons I learned during my early years in business were products of mistakes. Often, these are the lessons we remember best.

Learning in entrepreneurship goes beyond the acquisition of theoretical knowledge. It encompasses a growth mindset, where individuals consistently seek out new experiences, challenges, and perspectives. The more we learn, the more quickly we can move onto studying more complex or nuanced topics that can bring benefit to our businesses. The ability to adapt and learn from diverse situations fosters innovation, resilience, and flexibility—the essential traits that drive entrepreneurial success.

5. Business Strategy

A successful entrepreneur is commonly associated with building a prosperous company. Interestingly, however, business strategy ranks as the fifth most crucial skill among the entrepreneur's skill set. Rather than solely relying on this specific skill, entrepreneurs often achieve success through their unwavering determination and persistence. However, while entrepreneurs can adapt and learn business strategy on the go by employing effective communication, sales, focus, and learning abilities, it is essential to establish a strong foundation rooted in sound business sense and skills when structuring and expanding a business. To propel their ventures from a state of mediocrity to excellence, a successful entrepreneur must possess a well-defined and effective strategy. Entrepreneurs must think strategically and have a long-term vision for their business. They should be able to analyze market trends, identify opportunities and risks, and develop effective strategies to achieve their objectives.

DON'T FORGET...

Achieving success as an entrepreneur is not a simple equation, but those who thrive in this role often exhibit a mastery of specific skills. The five skills we looked at above sit atop this perch. However, there are various others that it would be unwise to overlook. I dedicate a few words to several of these below.

- ✓ **Leadership:** Entrepreneurs need strong leadership skills to inspire and motivate their team. They must set the direction, delegate tasks effectively, and provide guidance to their employees.
- ✓ **Creativity and Innovation:** Entrepreneurs often face problems that require creative solutions. Being able to think outside the box,

generate innovative ideas, and adapt to changing market trends is crucial for staying ahead of the competition.

- ✓ **Financial Literacy:** Understanding financial concepts and being able to interpret financial statements is crucial in business. Financial literacy involves knowledge of budgeting, forecasting, financial analysis, cash flow management, and the ability to make informed financial decisions. It is vital for entrepreneurs, managers, and anyone involved in financial roles.
- ✓ **Networking:** Building a strong network of contacts can open doors to opportunities, partnerships, and resources. Entrepreneurs should actively network, attend industry events, and cultivate relationships with other professionals in their field.
- ✓ **Adaptability:** In a rapidly changing business environment, being adaptable is crucial. Entrepreneurs must be open to new ideas, embrace technology, and be willing to pivot their strategies when necessary.
- ✓ **Time Management:** Entrepreneurs often have multiple responsibilities and limited time. Effective time management skills, prioritization, and the ability to delegate tasks are essential for maximizing productivity and achieving goals.
- ✓ **Customer Focus:** Understanding customers' needs and delivering value is paramount for success. Entrepreneurs should be able to listen to customer feedback, adapt their products or services accordingly, and provide exceptional customer experiences.
- ✓ **Technological Literacy:** In today's digital age, having a basic understanding of technology and digital tools is crucial. This includes proficiency in using productivity software, online collaboration tools, data analysis tools, and an understanding of emerging technologies relevant to the business.

While these abilities are of great significance, it is crucial to acknowledge that triumph in entrepreneurship is equally reliant on individual attributes such as passion, commitment, and a receptive attitude towards learning and self-improvement. Nurturing these proficiencies and traits demands dedication and time, yet they substantially amplify an entrepreneur's likelihood of attaining their aspirations. Our focus now shifts to an exploration of these aspects.

PERSONAL QUALITIES OF AN ENTREPRENEUR

Apart from developing and refining technical skills, the importance of personal qualities, often referred to as "soft skills," cannot be overstated. Building positive relationships and being pleasant to work with are crucial, since likability and friendliness are key to influencing others' willingness to collaborate or partner with us. Additionally, possessing creativity, adaptability, and resilience greatly contribute to navigating significant challenges effectively. The personal qualities of a good entrepreneur can vary to a noteworthy extent depending on the specific industry and individual circumstances. However, there are several key qualities that are generally considered important for entrepreneurial success in any realm. Let us overview some of these traits.

- ✓ **Passion and Motivation:** Entrepreneurs are often driven by a deep passion for their ideas or the industry they are entering. They possess a strong intrinsic motivation that fuels their determination to overcome challenges and pursue their goals. A passion for financial gain alone is, perhaps surprisingly, not enough. It is a passion for our work that truly shines through.
- ✓ **Self-Confidence:** Entrepreneurs must have confidence in themselves and their abilities. They need to believe in their vision and be able to inspire confidence in others, including investors, employees, and customers. If we do not believe in ourselves, we will have a tough time convincing others!
- ✓ **Strong Work Ethic:** Entrepreneurship demands hard work, long hours, and a high level of commitment. Good entrepreneurs are willing to put in the effort required to turn their ideas into reality. They lead by example and are not afraid to get their hands dirty.
- ✓ **Adaptability and Flexibility:** The business landscape is constantly evolving, and entrepreneurs need to be adaptable to changes in the

market, technology, and consumer preferences. They are open-minded and willing to adjust their strategies as needed.

- ✓ **Emotional Intelligence:** Emotional intelligence refers to the ability to recognize and manage one's own emotions and understand others' emotions. It involves self-awareness, empathy, relationship management, and the ability to navigate social dynamics effectively. Emotional intelligence enhances leadership, communication, and conflict resolution skills.
- ✓ **Risk-taking and Tolerance for Uncertainty:** Entrepreneurship involves taking calculated risks and being willing to make decisions in uncertain situations. Good entrepreneurs have a healthy tolerance for risk and are willing to step out of their comfort zones to pursue opportunities.

While these personal qualities can contribute to entrepreneurial success, note that none of us possesses all of them in equal measure. Each entrepreneur has their own unique strengths and weaknesses, and success often comes from a combination of personal qualities, experience, and the ability to learn and adapt along the way.

ENTREPRENEURIAL EDUCATION AND CAREER OUTLOOK

Becoming a successful entrepreneur requires a combination of innate abilities and acquired skills. While some talents may come naturally, others can be developed through training and education in the field of business and management. Academically speaking, pursuing a Master of Business Administration (MBA) is perhaps the most popular pathway for honing these skills. MBA coursework covers a wide range of essential business topics such as accounting, statistics, economics, communications, management, and entrepreneurship. By enrolling in an MBA program, individuals not only gain the necessary expertise to work in financial institutions but also equip themselves for leadership roles and even as founders of startup ventures.

Should you hold the conviction that you embody the indispensable traits for entrepreneurial achievement, it remains crucial to bear in mind that despite ingenious concepts and proficient management squads, unforeseen shifts in the market, fierce competition, or adverse conditions can potentially result in setbacks. The Small Business Administration reports that approximately 33% of startups do not survive beyond two years, 50% close within the fifth year, and 66% cease to exist by their tenth year. However, these statistics should not discourage you. If initial attempts fail to yield your desired outcomes, it is crucial to remain resilient and persistent. Embrace failure as an opportunity for learning and growth and be willing to try again.

GIVING BACK TO THE COMMUNITY

The act of giving back to the community is of utmost importance for organizations. While some may view it as an unnecessary burden, it is imperative for businesses to recognize their role and responsibility as an integral part of the community in which they operate. Without the support and patronage of community members, organizations would not exist. Therefore, it is essential for businesses to invest in the betterment of their community in order to create a symbiotic relationship with their customers.

By giving back to the community, organizations—both small startups and national corporations—not only improve their image but also enhance their brand reputation. When businesses actively participate in charitable activities or social initiatives, it demonstrates their commitment to social responsibility, which resonates positively with the public. This helps build goodwill and brand loyalty, as customers are more likely to support organizations that align with their values and contribute to the betterment of society.

Moreover, and on a more humanistic level, giving back to the community is simply the right thing to do. As members of society, organizations have a moral obligation to help those in need and contribute to the welfare of their community. By actively engaging in philanthropy, organizations demonstrate empathy, compassion, and a genuine concern for the well-being of others.

As a business owner myself, I have had the privilege of organizing and participating in various community-oriented events such as coat drives, food drives, and charity programs. While the primary motivation for my involvement is not for branding purposes, I have—as a byproduct of this generosity—received numerous compliments and positive feedback regarding my organization's charitable endeavors. These experiences have reinforced my belief that it is essential for businesses to elevate the communities they operate in and create more opportunities for the people who support them.

BENEFITS TO THE ORGANIZATION

Giving back to the community can improve an organization's image in several ways:

1. **Enhanced reputation:** By actively engaging in philanthropic activities, an organization demonstrates that it is committed to making a positive impact in the community. This fosters a good reputation and builds trust among customers, employees, investors, and other stakeholders.

2. **Positive brand association:** Community involvement projects create opportunities for the organization to align its brand with causes that resonate with people. This association helps to create a positive brand image and generates goodwill, as customers often prefer to support socially responsible companies.

3. **Increased customer loyalty:** When customers observe an organization actively participating in charitable activities, they feel a connection and become more loyal to the brand. Consumers are more likely to choose products or services from a company that gives back to the community over a competitor that does not.

4. **Attraction and retention of top talent:** Employees, especially the younger generations, increasingly value corporate social

responsibility. Organizations that prioritize community engagement are more attractive to potential employees. Existing employees are also more likely to remain engaged and committed when they see their company making a positive impact.

5. **Strengthened relationships with stakeholders:** Giving back to the community can strengthen relationships with stakeholders such as local government, regulatory bodies, NGOs, and industry associations. Organizations that actively participate in community initiatives are more likely to receive support, cooperation, and favorable treatment from these stakeholders.

6. **Positive media coverage:** Engaging in community initiatives often generates positive media attention. Media outlets are more likely to cover stories and events related to organizations that contribute positively to the community. Such coverage can significantly increase public awareness and promote a positive image for the organization.

7. **Differentiation from competitors:** In a competitive marketplace, a strong commitment to community involvement can help an organization stand out from its competitors. Customers and stakeholders may be more inclined to choose a company that supports the community over one that solely focuses on profit.

Overall, giving back to the community can significantly improve an organization's image by showcasing its commitment to social responsibility, building trust, and attracting loyal customers and talented employees.

CHAPTER TWO

IS THERE A NEED?

Commencing a business venture entail much more than simply unlocking the doors to sell or produce any arbitrary product. It transcends the mere notion of becoming a business owner. Instead, it necessitates the identification of a genuine need for the service or product being offered. This can involve filling a market gap that has yet to be satisfied or may mean introducing a superior approach to the current best-in-class. Whenever we examine the success stories of thriving corporations like Netflix, Amazon, Uber, and 7-Eleven, it becomes evident that they all did one of these two things. That is, they either tapped into a void or brought something unique to the table.

Let's break this down further. Amazon, the global e-commerce powerhouse founded in Jeff Bezos's garage, began by recognizing a need for a more convenient and accessible way to shop. Adapting to the emerging internet development of the 1990s, Amazon revolutionized the retail landscape by offering an extensive range of products online, complete with efficient delivery services. By identifying and fulfilling this need, Amazon not only transformed the way people shop but also established itself as a trusted and dominant player in the industry.

Likewise, Netflix revolutionized the entertainment industry by introducing a convenient streaming platform that disrupted the traditional model of renting or purchasing physical copies of movies and TV shows. With a vast library of content accessible at users' fingertips, Netflix capitalized on the growing demand for on-demand entertainment and forever changed the way people consume media.

Uber essentially took these same principles—convenience, cost-effectiveness and reliability—and used them to revolutionize the transportation industry by leveraging technology to connect riders with drivers. By recognizing the need for a seamless and efficient transportation solution, Uber capitalized on emerging technologies to transform the way people travel within cities, leading to its widespread adoption and global success.

Even 7-Eleven, a ubiquitous convenience store chain, found success by recognizing the need for accessible and convenient shopping options outside of traditional business hours. By offering round-the-clock service, 7-Eleven addressed the demands of a changing lifestyle and became a go-to destination for consumers seeking convenience and essential supplies at any time. Today, it boasts almost 80,000 stores spread across 19 countries around the globe.

In essence, the success of these notable corporations underscores the importance of identifying market needs, providing innovative, cutting-edge solutions, and meeting customer demands. By understanding the existing gaps or introducing unique propositions, businesses can carve their path to prosperity and become enduring players in their respective industries.

Brainstorming

When exploring potential business ventures, it is essential to engage in a thoughtful brainstorming process that takes into accounts your unique interests and skills. By aligning your business ideas with your personal passions, you can ensure a deep sense of purpose and fulfillment throughout your entrepreneurial journey. Furthermore, consider the process of pinpointing issues that genuinely ignite your passion. This entails an exploration of the diverse obstacles encountered by individuals or sectors, followed by the pursuit of solutions that eliminate these concerns. Furthermore, through a thorough examination of the market, the recognition of voids or unfulfilled requisites can unveil prospects for innovation that enable you to become first to market. Ultimately, by expanding your horizons and thinking creatively, you can uncover untapped niches and develop business ideas that have the potential for success and impact. Brainstorming is the first chapter of any successful business.

Market Research

When embarking on a new venture, it is crucial to conduct comprehensive research to not only assess the viability of your idea but also to identify potential customers who will embrace your product or service. Market research entails a multifaceted approach, including in-depth analysis of current market trends, meticulous identification of your target audience, and a thorough evaluation of your competition. By delving into these aspects, you gain valuable insights that enable you to make informed decisions and develop strategies that truly propel your business forward.

Understanding market trends empowers you to adapt to evolving consumer preferences and seize emerging opportunities, ensuring your idea aligns with the latest market demands. Identifying your target audience allows you to tailor your product or service to their specific needs and preferences, enhancing its appeal and fostering customer loyalty. Evaluating your competition, meanwhile, provides a deeper understanding of their strengths, weaknesses, and market positioning, enabling you to differentiate your offering and capitalize on untapped market segments. Overall, conducting comprehensive market research serves as a solid foundation for your business, helping you navigate the complexities of the marketplace with confidence and increasing your chances of long-term success.

Identify the Problem

The problem I am solving is multifaceted and encompasses several critical aspects of our modern lives. In today's fast-paced and information-driven world, we face numerous challenges when it comes to accessing, processing, and effectively utilizing the vast amount of data available to us. This information overload can be overwhelming, making it difficult for individuals and organizations to find the accurate and relevant information they need in a timely manner.

Additionally, effective communication has become increasingly crucial as we navigate complex societal and technological landscapes. Whether it's conveying ideas, understanding others, or bridging language barriers, clear and meaningful communication is vital for personal, professional, and global interactions.

The problem I am addressing is the need for a reliable and intelligent system that can efficiently retrieve information and facilitate effective communication. By harnessing the power of language models and natural language processing, I aim to provide individuals and organizations with a tool that can navigate the vast sea of information, filter out noise, and deliver accurate and relevant insights.

Refine your ideas

Refining ideas is a crucial step in the creative process that allows for the development and improvement of initial concepts. Whether you are working on a project, planning an event, or brainstorming new solutions, taking the time to refine your ideas can greatly enhance their effectiveness and quality. It will be useful for us to create a step-by-step approach to this:

1. **Clarify your objective:** Start by clearly defining your objective or goal. What is it that you want to achieve with your ideas? Having a clear focus will help guide your refinement process and ensure that your ideas remain aligned with your overall purpose.
2. **Evaluate feasibility:** Assess the feasibility of your ideas. Consider the resources, time, and skills required to execute them successfully. Be realistic about what is achievable within your limitations and make necessary adjustments to your ideas accordingly.
3. **Conduct research:** Gather relevant information and conduct research that support your ideas (potential investors will invariably want to see this; think back to the *Sharks* from Chapter One! This will oftentimes involve studying existing solutions, market trends, or gathering data that can validate or inspire your concepts. Research provides valuable insights and helps you refine your ideas with a well-informed perspective.
4. **Generate alternatives:** Brainstorm alternative approaches or variations to your initial ideas. This allows for exploration and encourages creativity. Do not hesitate to explore beyond conventional boundaries and entertain unconventional prospects. Sometimes, the best ideas emerge from unexpected places.

5. **Prioritize and select:** Review and prioritize your refined ideas based on their potential impact, feasibility, and alignment with your objectives. Consider the resources, time, and constraints you have, and select the ideas that have the highest potential for success.
6. **Refine the details:** Once you have selected your optimal ideas, it is time to delve deeper into the details. Break them down into smaller components and refine each aspect. Consider how each element contributes to your overall idea and make adjustments that enhance cohesiveness, functionality, or aesthetics.
7. **Seek feedback:** Share your refined ideas with others and seek feedback. Getting input from different perspectives can help identify potential issues, gaps, or areas for improvement. Sometimes, we can become so immersed in our ideas that it can be hard to see their drawbacks. Listen to constructive criticism and use it to iterate and refine your ideas further.
8. **Iterate and revise:** Refinement is an iterative—and often lengthy—process. Be open to revising and iterating on your ideas based on feedback and new insights. It may be tempting to overlook certain feedback in order to save time, but this can lead to regret when a potential investor points out the same criticism. Continually refine and improve until you feel that your ideas are well-developed and ready to be executed with confidence.
9. **Test and validate:** Whenever possible, test your refined ideas before implementing them on a larger scale. This can involve running pilot projects, conducting user testing, or gathering feedback from a small sample audience. Testing helps identify any remaining flaws or areas for improvement, allowing you to make final refinements.
10. **Document your ideas:** Finally, document your refined ideas in a clear and organized manner. This ensures that you capture the essence of your refined concepts and makes it easier to communicate and share them with others involved in the implementation process.

Remember, refining ideas takes time and effort. Embrace the process and allow yourself to explore different possibilities. With each iteration, your ideas will become sharper, more effective, and better aligned with your goals.

UNDERSTANDING THE CONCEPT OF NEED

Understanding the concept of need is fundamental to our understanding of human behavior, motivation, and the dynamics of society. Need refers to a condition or a requirement that is essential for an individual's well-being, satisfaction, or survival. It encompasses a wide range of physical, psychological, and social factors that influence our thoughts, emotions, and actions.

Human needs can be categorized into several dimensions. One of the most well-known frameworks is Maslow's Hierarchy of Needs, first proposed in 1943 by psychologist Abraham Maslow. According to this theory, our human needs are organized in a hierarchical structure, where lower-level needs must be satisfied before higher-level needs can be pursued. The hierarchy includes five main levels: physiological needs (such as food, water, and shelter), safety needs (including personal security, employment, and health), belongingness and love need (social relationships, affection, and acceptance), esteem needs (self-esteem, recognition, and achievement), and self-actualization needs (the realization of one's full potential and personal growth).

Beyond the framework of Maslow's Hierarchy, other scholars have expanded on the understanding of human needs. Psychologist Clayton Alderfer proposed the Existence, Relatedness, and Growth theory, which categorizes needs into three broad categories: existence needs (material and physiological well-being), relatedness needs (social relationships and interpersonal connections), and growth needs (personal development and self-actualization). This theory suggests that these three categories of needs can operate simultaneously and that frustration in one category may lead individuals to seek satisfaction in another.

Another influential perspective comes from self-determination theory, developed by psychologists Edward Deci and Richard Ryan. SDT proposes that humans have three innate psychological needs: autonomy (the need to experience volition and self-direction), competence (the need to feel effective and capable), and relatedness (the need to connect and form meaningful relationships with others). According to SDT, these needs are essential for intrinsic motivation and well-being. If you wish to take some time researching this interesting field further, you may also wish to seek information on David McClelland's *Need Theory* and Manfred Max-Neef's *Human Scale Development.*

Importantly for our entrepreneurial journey, the concept of needs extends to economic theory. In economics, *needs* are often distinguished from *wants*. While needs refer to the goods and services necessary for survival and basic wellbeing, wants are desires for inessential goods and services that enhance individuals' quality of life. Understanding the distinction between needs and wants is essential for economic analysis, resource allocation, and market dynamics. It is worth noting here too that cultural and societal factors significantly influence our perception and prioritization of needs. What is considered a basic need in one society may be seen as a luxury or irrelevant in another. For example, access to clean water and sanitation is universally recognized as a basic need, yet the specific cultural, economic, and environmental contexts shape the strategies and solutions used to meet this need across different societies. This is one of the reasons why conducting cross-cultural market research is essential before making plans to expand your business overseas.

Finally, the concept of needs is not static. It evolves over time due to advancements in technology, changes in social norms, and shifts in individuals' aspirations and expectations. For instance, as societies progress, needs related to information, education, and access to technology become increasingly important. This in turn has opened an abundance of new commercial opportunities, often embraced lucratively by who's capable of adapting and responding quickly.

FACTORS INFLUENCING THE PERCEPTION OF NEED

The perception of need is influenced by a variety of factors, ranging from individual characteristics and experiences to societal and cultural influences. These factors play a significant role in shaping how individuals perceive their needs and prioritize them. Understanding these factors can provide valuable insights into human behavior, decision-making processes, and the dynamics of consumerism. Below are several crucial factors that impact the way needs are perceived:

- **Personal Experiences:** Personal experiences have a profound impact on how individuals perceive their needs. Past experiences, both positive and negative, shape our understanding of what we require to lead a fulfilling life. For example, someone who has experienced financial instability in the past may prioritize financial security as a fundamental need, whereas someone who has never faced such challenges may not perceive it as strongly. This person-to-person variation is hard to cater for as an entrepreneur, but it can help channel our research to understand what portion of our potential market may have been impacted by certain events.
- **Social and Cultural Influences:** As mentioned above, social and cultural factors significantly shape our perception of need. Societal norms, values, and expectations influence what we consider essential for a good life. For instance, in some cultures, owning a car may be seen as a necessity for transportation, while in others, public transportation or bicycles may be considered sufficient. Similarly, societal pressure and media influence can create artificial needs, such as the desire for certain brands or luxury goods. Again, understanding and responsibilities to these can help us identify our target market and decide upon potential expansion plans.
- **Psychological Factors:** Psychological factors—such as personality traits, self-esteem, and aspirations—impact how individuals perceive their needs. For instance, individuals with high self-esteem may prioritize the need for self-actualization and personal growth, whereas those with low self-esteem may prioritize the need for validation and social acceptance.

- **Economic Factors:** Economic circumstances, including income level, financial resources, and availability of goods and services, play a significant role in shaping the perception of need. Higher income individuals may have more resources to fulfill their needs and may perceive certain goods and services as essential, whereas individuals with limited financial means may have a narrower perception of their needs due to financial constraints. Naturally, this has implications for us as entrepreneurs.
- **Environmental Factors:** The physical environment in which individuals live can influence their perception of need. Factors such as climate, geography, urban or rural settings, and access to resources can impact what individuals consider necessary for their well-being. For example, someone living in a cold climate may prioritize the need for warm clothing and heating, whereas someone in a tropical region may prioritize the need for air conditioning.
- **Marketing and Advertising:** Marketing and advertising techniques play a crucial, often decisive, role in shaping the perception of need. Through persuasive messaging and strategic branding, marketers create a sense of desire and urgency, convincing individuals that certain products or services are indispensable for their well-being or happiness. This influence can sometimes distort individuals' perception of their true needs.

It is important to note that the perception of need is subjective and can vary significantly from person to person. These factors provide a general framework for understanding how individuals perceive their needs, but individual circumstances and personal preferences ultimately determine the importance and prioritization of specific needs.

ASSESSING THE EXISTENCE OF NEED

Assessing the existence of need is a critical task in various domains, including social sciences, public policy, healthcare, and—most pertinently for us—business. This process involves determining whether a particular need or problem exists within a given context or population, typically through collecting and analyzing data to gain insights into the nature, extent, and severity of the need. This information is crucial for making informed decisions, allocating resources effectively, and developing appropriate interventions or solutions.

The assessment of need begins with recognizing the importance of understanding the specific problem or requirement under consideration. In business terms, acknowledging the existence of need is the first step towards finding viable solutions for current issues within the market. Without a comprehensive assessment, we may overlook critical problems or misdirect our resources, leading to ineffective or inefficient outcomes.

One of the key aspects of assessing need is defining and delineating the scope of the problem. This involves clearly specifying the boundaries and parameters of the need, such as the target population, geographical area, time frame, and relevant variables. A well-defined scope helps to focus the assessment process, ensuring that efforts are directed towards gathering relevant data and conducting appropriate analyses. Of course, the scope of the problem correlates directly with the size of our potential customer base. As such, it is vital that we obtain an accurate (or as accurate as possible) figure.

Various methods and tools can be deployed to determine the existence and magnitude of need, depending on the nature of the problem and available resources. Quantitative approaches, such as surveys, questionnaires, and statistical analysis, provide numerical data that can help quantify the extent of the need. Qualitative methods, such as interviews, focus groups, and case studies, offer insights into the lived experiences, perspectives, and narratives of individuals or communities affected by the need. Combining these approaches can provide a more comprehensive understanding of the problem, offering a holistic view of the need.

Data collection in need assessment often involves both primary and secondary sources. Primary data refers to information gathered directly from the target population or through firsthand observations of our potential customers. This can involve us conducting surveys, interviews, or observations in the field, and statistically analyzing the data we collect. Secondary data, on the other hand, refers to existing data collected by other researchers, organizations, or government agencies. This may include data from published reports, databases, or previous studies. Tools such as Google Scholar can be priceless resources in helping us locate and access such papers, which in turn can provide much-needed statistical evidence of our customer base or market gap. By utilizing both primary and secondary data, researchers can cross-validate findings, enhance the reliability of results, and uncover additional insights.

However, it is important to acknowledge that assessing the existence of need is not a purely objective or value-neutral process. The interpretation of data and the determination of need can be influenced by various factors, including the researcher's biases, the framing of the research question, and the contextual factors surrounding the assessment. Therefore, it is crucial to approach the assessment process with transparency, rigor, and openness to diverse perspectives.

Furthermore, the assessment of need is an iterative and ongoing process. Our customers' needs can evolve over time, and new challenges may arise that require reevaluation and reassessment. Regular monitoring and evaluation of the identified need are essential to ensure that the services and solutions we provide remain effective and responsive to the changing circumstances. Products can quickly become outdated if we fail to pay attention to the dynamic development of consumer needs.

In summary, assessing the existence of need—a vital step of all market research—is a complex and multifaceted endeavor. It requires careful consideration of the problem's scope, the use of appropriate data collection methods, rigorous analysis, and interpretation of findings. By undertaking a thorough assessment, decision-makers can gain valuable insights into the nature and extent of the need, enabling them to develop targeted interventions, allocate resources efficiently, and ultimately make a positive impact on the lives of individuals and communities.

EVALUATING THE NEED FOR CHANGE

Evaluating the need for change is an essential process for individuals, organizations, and societies to assess whether existing systems, practices, or circumstances require modification. Change can be driven by various factors, such as advancements in technology, shifts in market dynamics, social or cultural transformations, or personal growth and development. By evaluating the need for change, individuals and entities can determine whether current approaches are still effective, identify areas that require improvement, and devise strategies to adapt and thrive in an ever-evolving world.

One of the key reasons for evaluating the need for change is to ensure relevance and competitiveness. In a rapidly changing environment, organizations must continually assess their products, services, and internal processes to meet the evolving needs and expectations of their customers. This evaluation allows them to stay ahead of the competition, identify emerging trends, and take proactive measures to remain relevant in the market.

Moreover, evaluating the need for change helps identify inefficiencies and areas of improvement. It provides an opportunity to critically analyze existing processes, systems, or structures and identify bottlenecks or areas that hinder productivity or hinder progress. By evaluating these areas, organizations and individuals can streamline operations, eliminate redundancies, and enhance overall efficiency, leading to cost savings and improved outcomes.

Another significant aspect of evaluating the need for change is to address emerging risks and challenges. As new technologies, regulations, or external factors emerge, they can create risks or threats that may impact the stability or success of an organization. By conducting a thorough evaluation, individuals and entities can proactively identify potential risks, assess their impact, and develop contingency plans or mitigation strategies to minimize adverse effects.

Furthermore, evaluating the need for change fosters innovation and fosters a culture of continuous improvement. It encourages individuals and organizations to think critically, challenge the status quo, and seek innovative solutions to address existing problems or seize new opportunities. By fostering a culture of change and innovation, individuals and organizations can adapt more readily to external disruptions and remain agile in an ever-changing world.

Evaluating the need for change also plays a vital role in personal growth and development. As individuals, we go through different stages in life, and our goals, aspirations, and circumstances change over time. By periodically evaluating our lives, careers, or relationships, we can identify areas that require attention, set new goals, and make necessary adjustments to align our lives with our evolving values and aspirations. This process enables personal growth, enhances well-being, and facilitates a sense of fulfillment and satisfaction.

Overall, evaluating the need for change is a crucial process for individuals, organizations, and societies. It helps to ensure relevance and competitiveness, identify inefficiencies and areas of improvement, address emerging risks and challenges, foster innovation, and promote personal growth and development. By embracing change and conducting regular evaluations, individuals and entities can adapt to the dynamic nature of the world and position themselves for success in an ever-evolving landscape.

CHAPTER THREE

BUSINESS MANAGEMENT-CUSTOMER SERVICE-PAYROLL

Being in business for over 20 years has provided me with a wealth of experience and insights into the complexities of managing other people. Throughout this journey, I have come to realize that managing individuals is undeniably one of the most challenging tasks that any person can undertake. We cannot approach management without flexibility. Quite the opposite, each person that we involve without business will possess a unique set of qualities, strengths, and weaknesses that demand a tailored approach. There is no 'one-size-fits-all' when it comes to effective team management.

I have encountered a diverse array of characters within the workforce of my company. There were those who demonstrated opportunistic tendencies, always seeking personal gain, and there were others who played the role of geniuses, consistently displaying exceptional skills and intellect. We cannot divide our time equally between every employee, of course. This is where the implementation of set rules and guidelines, ones that apply to personnel throughout your entire company, take center stage.

Maintaining a set of rules ensures consistency and fairness in the workplace, acting as an anchor for both management and employees alike. Deviating from these rules to accommodate individuals often creates imbalance within the organization. It creates an environment where favoritism and arbitrariness prevail, eroding trust and fostering discontent. Consequently, the overall functioning of the company suffers, hindering productivity and jeopardizing the achievement of organizational goals.

It should become evident, then, that it is balance adaptability with a capacity to enforce strict rules where needed. To overcome this challenge in my own entrepreneurial career, I have worked tirelessly to hone my skills in understanding individual differences and—as far as is possible—tailoring my approach accordingly. Getting to know your employees is paramount. Employing active listening, empathy, and open communication fosters a supportive environment in which individuals feel valued and acknowledged. Over the years, I have found that adjusting my management style to cater to each employee's unique requirements has not only enhanced their development but also fostered a harmonious and productive atmosphere.

DEFINING BUSINESS MANAGEMENT

Business management refers to the process of planning, organizing, directing, and controlling the resources and activities of an organization to achieve its goals effectively and efficiently. It involves overseeing various aspects of a business, including strategy formulation, resource allocation, decision-making, employee coordination, and performance evaluation. The primary objective of business management is to optimize the use of available resources and create a sustainable competitive advantage to ensure the long-term success and growth of the organization.

SCOPE OF BUSINESS MANAGEMENT

The scope of business management is broad, encompassing various functional areas and activities within an organization. Some key components include:

- **Strategic Management:** This involves setting the long-term vision, mission, and goals of the organization, and devising strategies to achieve them. Strategic management involves analyzing the external environment, identifying opportunities and threats, and aligning the organization's resources to capitalize on its strengths and overcome weaknesses.

- **Operations Management:** This focuses on designing, controlling, and improving the processes and systems that deliver goods or services to customers. Operations management involves optimizing production, managing supply chains, ensuring quality control, and improving overall efficiency.
- **Financial Management:** Financial management is concerned with the management of financial resources, including budgeting, financial planning, financial analysis, and capital allocation. It aims to ensure the organization's financial health and stability.
- **Marketing Management:** Marketing management involves identifying customer needs, developing products or services that meet those needs, and creating approaches for pricing, promotion, and distribution. It aims to create and maintain a positive brand image and attract and retain customers, aiding both short- and long-term success.
- **Human Resource Management:** This focuses on managing the organization's workforce, including recruitment, selection, training, performance appraisal, compensation, and employee relations. Human resource management aims to develop a skilled and motivated workforce to achieve organizational objectives.
- **Information Technology Management:** IT management deals with the effective use and implementation of technology within the organization. It includes managing IT infrastructure, software applications, data security, and digital transformation initiatives.
- **Risk Management:** Risk management involves identifying and mitigating potential risks that could impact the organization's performance or reputation. It includes risk assessment, risk analysis, and the development of risk management strategies.
- **Entrepreneurship and Innovation:** Business management also encompasses fostering a culture of innovation and entrepreneurship within the organization. This involves encouraging creativity, seeking new opportunities, and adapting to changes in the business environment.
- **Ethics and Corporate Social Responsibility:** Business management involves making ethical decisions and promoting responsible business

practices that consider the impact of the organization's activities on society and the environment.

Overall, the scope of business management is dynamic and evolving, adapting to changes in the business landscape and incorporating new concepts and practices to ensure the organization's success and sustainability.

HOW TO MANAGE A BUSINESS

Managing a business is a multifaceted task that requires a combination of strategic planning, effective leadership, and adaptability to succeed in a competitive market. Whether you, the reader, consider yourself to be a seasoned entrepreneur or a first timer, mastering the art of business management is essential for long-term success. Drawing on my decades of experience, I have identified five indispensable steps that—if navigated successfully—will set your business up for success.

- **Develop a Clear Vision and Plan:** Every successful business is founded around a clear vision and well-defined goals. Think back to the Amazon, Netflix, 7-Eleven and Uber examples we discussed earlier. Thus, you must create a comprehensive business plan that outlines your target market, marketing strategy, financial projections, and operational processes. Having a roadmap will keep you focused and provide direction for your team. Regularly review and update your plan to adapt to changing market conditions and business needs.
- **Cultivate Effective Leadership:** As a business owner or manager, your leadership skills play a crucial role in guiding your team towards success. Lead by example, inspire your employees, and encourage open communication. Create a positive work culture that fosters collaboration and innovation. Recognize and reward your team's efforts to boost morale and motivation. Effective leadership will not only improve productivity in the short-term but also enhance employee retention and satisfaction, leading to long-term stability and achievement.

- **Manage Finances Wisely:** Proper financial management is vital for the survival and growth of any business. Monitor your cash flow regularly, ensuring you have enough funds to cover expenses and investments. Keep a close eye on your financial statements, analyze trends, and identify areas where you can cut costs or improve revenue. If you feel uncomfortable managing your own finances—or if you feel as though you lack the training or mathematical skills needed to do so—you may consider working with an accountant or financial advisor to make informed decisions and maintain financial stability. This does not have to be costly, especially if you take advantage of the burgeoning 'gig economy', and it can save you a great deal in both time and worry.
- **Embrace Technology and Innovation:** In today's digital age, technology plays a pivotal role in business success. Embrace technological advancements that can streamline your operations, improve your customers' experience, and boost your overall efficiency. From implementing cloud-based software for better collaboration to utilizing data analytics for informed decision-making, integrating technology will give your business a competitive edge.
- **Adapt and Stay Agile:** The business landscape is ever-changing, and adaptability is key to staying ahead of the curve. Be open to innovation and new ideas and be willing to pivot your strategies when necessary. Monitor industry trends, customer feedback, and competitors to identify opportunities and potential threats. Stay agile by empowering your team to be flexible and responsive to market changes.

In summary, business management demands careful planning, effective leadership, financial acumen, technological integration, and the ability to adapt to a dynamic environment. By developing a clear vision, cultivating strong leadership, managing finances wisely, embracing technology, and staying agile, you can position your business for long-term success and navigate the challenges of the ever-evolving market.

CUSTOMER SERVICE IN BUSINESS MANAGEMENT

Customer service is an integral aspect of any business, and something that many entrepreneurs have little-to-no experience with ahead of embarking on their first start-up venture. Dealing with difficult customers can be challenging, we have all seen social media videos showing some extreme examples, but it is critical that any business owner reacts fairly and professionally to every customer (even those who might not behave that way towards us). Every customer deserves to feel valued and appreciated for choosing to do business with you. Nonetheless, if you are in business long enough, you will eventually come across certain situations where you may need to politely inform a customer that their business would be better served elsewhere. Throughout my own experiences in customer service, I have encountered both positive and negative interactions. While I may not have always responded optimally, these encounters have taught me the importance of authenticity and respect towards my customers.

In the realm of customer service, it is inevitable that some customers may prove to be demanding or challenging. However, it is essential to maintain composure and professionalism, ensuring that each customer feels respected and appreciated. By doing so, we foster positive relationships and create an environment conducive to customer satisfaction. Nevertheless, there may arise instances where a customer's demands or behavior exceed reasonable limits. In such cases, it is important to politely and tactfully communicate that their best interests would be better served elsewhere. While this may mean that you are turning down financial gain in the short-term, this may well be outweighed by the headache that you save over a longer period! Maintaining open and honest communication while adhering to a professional demeanor is crucial in these situations.

Above all else, remember that customer service is a critical aspect of business management that *directly* impacts your company's success and reputation. Excellent customer service goes beyond merely resolving issues; it involves building strong relationships with customers, understanding their needs, and exceeding their expectations. In today's competitive market, companies that prioritize outstanding customer service gain a significant advantage over their competitors. Let us look at some of the ways that customer service can impact your business, be it a startup or a well-established brand, and how we can take steps to implement this.

IMPORTANCE OF CUSTOMER SERVICE

- **Customer Retention:** Happy and satisfied customers are more likely to become repeat patrons, making repeat purchases and staying loyal to the brand. Loyal customers also tend to recommend the business to others, which can lead to new customer acquisition. Some businesses may encourage such recommendations by setting up a referral program.
- **Brand Reputation:** Positive customer experiences lead to a positive reputation for the company. Word-of-mouth plays a crucial role in shaping a brand's image, and exceptional customer service can allow positive reviews to spread like wildfire.
- **Differentiation:** In industries where products or services are similar, exceptional customer service can be a key differentiator, especially in the reviews that we receive. It provides a competitive edge and can help your company stand out from the crowd.
- **Increased Revenue:** Customers who feel valued and well-served are more likely to spend more with our business. Upselling and cross-selling opportunities arise when customers have trust in the company and its offerings.
- **Customer Feedback and Improvement:** Engaging with customers through effective customer service channels allows businesses to gather feedback and identify areas for improvement. This feedback loop helps in refining products, services, and overall operations.

KEY COMPONENTS OF EXCELLENT CUSTOMER SERVICE

- ✓ **Communication:** Effective communication is the foundation of good customer service. Businesses must be responsive to inquiries, provide clear and accurate information, and maintain open channels of communication through a variety of platforms, including phone, email, chat, and social media.

- ✓ **Empathy:** Understanding and empathizing with customers' concerns and emotions are vital in creating a positive experience. Empathetic responses show that the business values its customers and cares about their well-being.
- ✓ **Personalization:** Treating customers as individuals, not just as a number, enhances the customer experience. Tailoring interactions based on their preferences, purchase history, and previous interactions shows that the business values each customer uniquely.
- ✓ **Timeliness:** Responding promptly to customer inquiries, resolving issues quickly, and delivering products or services on time are crucial for customer satisfaction.
- ✓ **Problem Solving:** Businesses should equip their customer service representatives with the necessary tools and authority to resolve customer issues efficiently. Empowering staff to make decisions fosters a sense of trust and satisfaction among customers.
- ✓ **Consistency:** Consistency in customer service across all touch points and throughout the customer journey is essential. Customers expect the same level of service from the first interaction to the last.
- ✓ **Continuous Improvement:** Customer service is not a static process; it requires continuous improvement based on feedback and changing customer needs. Regularly reviewing customer service metrics and implementing necessary changes is essential for growth.

IMPLEMENTING EFFECTIVE CUSTOMER SERVICE

- **Training:** Once your business is large enough to employ a dedicated customer service team, it is important that you properly train all representatives to handle various situations, use customer service tools effectively, and develop communication and problem-solving skills.
- **Technology:** Utilize customer service software and technology that streamlines interactions and allows for better tracking and management of customer inquiries.

- **Feedback Mechanisms:** Offer multiple avenues for customers to provide feedback, such as surveys, online reviews, or feedback forms. Act upon the feedback received to improve the overall customer experience.
- **Customer Service Policies:** Develop clear and customer-centric policies that guide interactions and ensure consistency across all customer touch points. Clear policies will also protect your employees and representatives on the occasions where a customer demands too much from them.
- **Customer-Centric Culture:** Foster a customer-centric culture within the organization, where all employees understand the importance of excellent customer service and are committed to delivering it.

Overall, in business management, customer service plays a pivotal role in fostering customer loyalty, brand reputation, and long-term success. Companies that prioritize and invest in exceptional customer service create a positive and memorable experience, leading to increased customer retention, enhanced brand image, and ultimately, higher revenue. By understanding the significance of customer service and implementing best practices, businesses can build lasting relationships with their customers and thrive in a competitive market.

PAYROLL MANAGEMENT IN BUSINESS MANAGEMENT

Payroll management is a fundamental element of business administration, encompassing the efficient handling of employee compensation, benefits, taxes, and deductions. Its significance lies in ensuring precise and prompt payment to employees while adhering to pertinent labor laws and tax regulations. Over the following pages, we will explore this in greater detail.

KEY COMPONENTS OF PAYROLL MANAGEMENT

- **Employee Information:** Payroll management begins with gathering essential employee information, such as names, addresses, tax withholding details, and bank account numbers. Maintaining accurate and up-to-date employee records is crucial for error-free payroll processing.
- **Time and Attendance Tracking**: Accurately tracking employees' work hours is essential for determining their compensation. This can be done through timekeeping systems, biometric devices, or electronic timecards.
- **Salary and Compensation Structure:** Payroll management involves calculating employees' salaries, wages, commissions, and bonuses based on their employment contracts or company policies.
- **Tax Calculation and Withholding:** Accurate calculation and withholding of income taxes, social security contributions, and other applicable deductions are essential to ensure compliance with tax laws.
- **Benefits Administration:** Payroll management includes managing employee benefits, such as health insurance, retirement plans, paid time off, and other similar perks.
- **Statutory Compliance:** Ensuring compliance with labor laws, tax regulations, and other government mandates is critical for avoiding penalties and maintaining your reputation.
- **Payroll Processing:** The actual payroll processing involves calculating net pay after deductions, generating pay stubs, and initiating salary transfers to employees' bank accounts.
- **Record Keeping:** Thorough and organized record keeping is essential for auditing purposes, as well as for providing your employees with historical payment information.

BEST PRACTICES IN PAYROLL MANAGEMENT

- **Reliable Payroll Software:** Implementing robust payroll software simplifies and automates payroll processes, reducing errors and saving time for HR personnel.

- **Regular Auditing:** Conduct periodic audits to verify the accuracy of payroll data and ensure compliance with regulations.
- **Stay Updated on Legal Changes:** Keep track of changes in tax laws, labor regulations, and employment policies to remain compliant and avoid legal issues.
- **Direct Deposit:** Offer direct deposit options to employees to streamline payment processes and improve convenience.
- **Data Security:** Safeguard payroll data to protect sensitive employee information from unauthorized access.
- **Timely Payroll Processing:** Adhere to strict payroll schedules to ensure employees are paid on time and without delays.
- **Communication with Employees:** Provide clear and transparent communication with employees regarding payroll-related matters, such as pay schedules, deductions, and benefits.
- **Training and Education:** Regularly train HR personnel involved in payroll management to keep them updated on best practices and compliance requirements.

BENEFITS OF EFFECTIVE PAYROLL MANAGEMENT

- **Employee Satisfaction:** Timely and accurate payrolls contribute to employee satisfaction and motivation, fostering a positive work environment.
- **Compliance and Risk Mitigation:** Proper payroll management ensures compliance with labor laws and tax regulations, reducing the risk of legal penalties.
- **Time and Cost Savings:** Automating payroll processes saves time for HR personnel, allowing them to focus on other strategic HR initiatives.
- **Improved Financial Planning:** Accurate payroll data aids in better financial planning and budgeting for the organization.
- **Enhanced Organizational Reputation:** Efficient payroll management reflects positively on the company's reputation, making it an attractive employer for potential candidates.

Taken as a whole, payroll management stands as a critical cornerstone within business administration, encompassing a spectrum of processes meticulously designed to guarantee precise and punctual employee compensation. The art of proficient payroll management entails the utilization of reliable software, adherence to legal mandates (remember, these may differ between jurisdictions), and an unwavering commitment to data security. Through the adoption of optimal methodologies and a dedication to effective payroll management, your business can elevate employee contentment, curtail potential liabilities, and make substantial strides toward realizing your dreams of prosperity.

TYPES OF DECISION IN BUSINESS MANAGEMENT

In business management, decisions play a crucial role in shaping your organization's success and growth. These decisions can be broadly categorized into various types based on their scope, level of impact, and nature. Here are the most common types of decision that you are certain to face:

- **Strategic Decisions:** These decisions are high-level and long-term in nature, aiming to define the overall direction and objectives of your organization. Strategic decisions involve choices such as market positioning, product development, geographic expansion, mergers and acquisitions, and resource allocation.
- **Tactical Decisions:** Tactical decisions are of medium-term importance and are typically made by middle-level managers. They are focused on implementing the strategies set by top management. Examples of tactical decisions include budgeting, workforce planning, inventory management, and marketing campaigns.
- **Operational Decisions:** These are the day-to-day decisions made by your front-line managers and employees to ensure smooth operations and efficient use of resources. Operational decisions may include production scheduling, quality control, supplier selection, and customer service management.

- **Programmed Decisions:** Programmed decisions are repetitive and routine, guided by established policies, rules, and procedures. These decisions are often automated and can be made using predefined criteria. Examples include inventory reorder points, routine maintenance schedules, and employee leave approvals.
- **Non-programmed Decisions**: Non-programmed arise in response to novel situations and uncertainties, thereby necessitating careful analyses and an evaluation of several possible solutions. Crisis management situations are perhaps the leading example of occurrences that would likely fall into this category.
- **Individual Decisions:** These decisions are made by a single person, such as a manager or business owner, without involving others in the decision-making process. Individual decisions are often quicker but may lack diverse perspectives.
- **Group Decisions:** Group decisions involve multiple stakeholders, managers, or teams working together to reach a consensus. They promote collaboration, diverse inputs, and better decision quality. However, group decisions may take longer to reach consensus.
- **Routine Decisions:** Routine decisions are made frequently and typically have a low impact on the organization. They may involve minor adjustments or straightforward choices that align with established procedures.
- **Policy Decisions:** Policy decisions involve setting guidelines, rules, and principles to guide future actions and decisions within the organization. These decisions provide a framework for handling various situations consistently.
- **Crisis Decisions:** Crisis decisions are made in response to unexpected and urgent situations that can significantly impact the organization's survival or reputation. They require quick thinking and decisive actions to address the crisis effectively.
- **Ethical Decisions:** Ethical decisions involve considering moral principles and values while making choices that may have ethical implications. Business managers often face ethical dilemmas and

need to weigh the consequences of their actions on stakeholders and society.

Each of these decision types plays a crucial role in managing a business effectively and navigating the challenges and opportunities in a dynamic market environment. Successful business management involves a balanced approach to making and implementing decisions at different levels and situations.

THE SYNERGY OF CUSTOMER SERVICE AND PAYROLL IN BUSINESS MANAGEMENT

In the constantly evolving realm of business management, we have seen how two fundamental elements emerge as essential cornerstones of success: customer service and payroll. Despite appearing superficially unrelated, the symbiotic relationship between these components can wield considerable influence over a company's performance and ultimate triumph. In this section, we delve into the profound implications that arise when customer service and payroll functions are aligned and integrated, fostering a seamless and productive business ecosystem.

- **Enhanced Employee Motivation and Satisfaction**

A well-organized payroll system that ensures timely and accurate salary payments fosters a positive work environment. Satisfied employees are more likely to provide exceptional customer service, as they feel valued and motivated to perform at their best. Conversely, a poorly managed payroll system can lead to discontent among employees, resulting in negative customer interactions. By linking payroll with customer service, businesses can recognize and reinforce the direct relationship between employee satisfaction and customer satisfaction.

- **Seamless Customer Experience**

Customer service and payroll share a common thread - both directly impact the customer experience. When customers encounter issues or have inquiries, they expect prompt and efficient responses from the customer service team. A smooth payroll system ensures that employees remain focused on their responsibilities, ultimately translating to improved customer interactions. By streamlining these processes and providing necessary resources, companies can create a seamless experience for both customers and employees.

- **Data-Driven Decision Making**

Integrating customer service and payroll data can provide valuable insights to business managers. By analyzing patterns in customer complaints or inquiries alongside payroll metrics such as employee turnover, companies can identify potential issues that impact both sides of the equation. This data-driven approach enables management to make informed decisions, leading to more effective resource allocation, targeted training, and improved overall performance.

- **Retaining Top Talent**

Payroll is not just about salary payments; it also encompasses employee benefits, rewards, and recognition programs. These aspects play a significant role in talent retention. Satisfied employees are more likely to stay with your company, reducing turnover costs and maintaining a knowledgeable and experienced workforce. In turn, this stability positively affects customer service as customers prefer interacting with familiar and experienced representatives who understand their needs and concerns.

- **Improving Customer Loyalty**

Outstanding customer service is the bedrock of customer loyalty. When customers feel valued and believe that their concerns are addressed promptly, they are more likely to remain loyal to your brand and recommend it to others. Payroll functions contribute indirectly to customer loyalty by fostering a content and engaged workforce, who, in turn, can deliver superior customer service consistently. This virtuous cycle strengthens the brand-customer relationship and enhances customer lifetime value.

- **Employee Training and Development**

Combining customer service and payroll insights can help identify areas where your employees might need additional training and development. For instance, if customer complaints indicate a recurring issue, you may wish to arrange targeted training that directly addresses this point. In tandem, recognizing exemplary customer service through appropriate recognition (many entrepreneurs choose to set up employee rewards schemes) can motivate employees to continually enhance their skills and knowledge.

Overall, the synergy between customer service and payroll in business management is undeniable. By recognizing their interdependence and integrating these functions strategically, companies can create a harmonious ecosystem that boosts employee morale, enhances customer experiences, and drives overall success. Empowered by data-driven decision-making and a commitment to employee satisfaction, businesses can strengthen their competitive edge and foster long-lasting customer relationships in today's dynamic marketplace.

PAYROLL PROCESSING, COMPLIANCE, AND LEGAL CONSIDERATIONS

Effective payroll processing is essential for any business to ensure timely and accurate payment to employees while adhering to relevant laws and regulations. Managing payroll involves various tasks, from calculating wages and deductions to ensuring compliance with local, state, and federal laws. In this article, we will explore the key aspects of payroll processing, compliance, and the legal considerations that businesses need to be aware of.

1. Payroll Processing:

Payroll processing refers to the steps taken by an organization to calculate and distribute employee compensation. It involves several stages, including:

- **Employee Information Collection:** Accurate employee data is fundamental for proper payroll processing. Companies must gather and maintain essential details such as employee names, addresses, Social Security numbers, tax withholding information, salary or hourly rate, benefits, and deductions.
- **Timekeeping and Attendance Tracking:** Accurate timekeeping processes are vital if employers are to calculate employees' wages correctly. Many businesses deploy timekeeping systems or software

that integrates with payroll processing to record employees' work hours and attendance.

- **Wage Calculation:** Depending on the employment terms (hourly wage, annual salary, etc.) and any overtime, paid time off, or other factors, the payroll team calculates the employees' gross wages.
- **Tax Withholding:** Employers must withhold federal, state, and local taxes from employees' paychecks. The amount withheld is based on the information provided by employees on their W-4 forms.
- **Deductions and Contributions:** Payroll processing includes calculating and deducting the appropriate amounts for covering employee benefits, retirement contributions, health insurance, and other such deductions.
- **Net Pay Distribution:** After all calculations and deductions are made, employees receive their net pay, which you will likely choose to administer through either direct deposit or physical paychecks.

2. Compliance:

Payroll compliance involves adhering to various legal and regulatory requirements set forth by governments and industry-specific authorities. Non-compliance can result in penalties, fines, or even legal actions. Key aspects of payroll compliance include:

- **Tax Compliance:** Accurate and timely payment of payroll taxes is crucial. Employers must stay updated with changing tax rates and laws to ensure proper withholding and reporting.
- **Employment Laws:** Compliance with labor laws, such as minimum wage, overtime, working hours, and child labor regulations, is essential to protect employees' rights and avoid legal issues.
- **Benefits and Deductions:** Employers must comply with regulations concerning employee benefits, such as healthcare and retirement plans, and ensure that deductions are made accurately and transparently.
- **Record Keeping:** Maintaining detailed payroll records is a legal requirement. Records should include employee data, pay rates,

timekeeping records, tax forms, and any other relevant documentation.

- **Reporting:** Employers must submit payroll-related reports to government agencies, such as quarterly and annual tax filings.

3. Legal Considerations:

In addition to compliance with specific regulations, you—as a business owner—should be aware of broader legal considerations related to payroll:

- **Data Security and Privacy:** Handling sensitive employee information requires strict data security measures to safeguard against data breaches and identity theft.
- **Payroll Discrepancies and Disputes:** Employers must have a well-defined process to address payroll discrepancies and employee disputes with speed and fairness.
- **Payroll Fraud Prevention:** Implementing internal controls and regular audits can help prevent payroll fraud and ensure accuracy.
- **State and Local Laws:** Payroll laws may vary from state to state and even at the local level. Businesses operating in multiple locations must be aware of and comply with the specific laws in each jurisdiction.

In summary, payroll processing, compliance, and legal considerations are vital aspects of running a business responsibly and ethically. Employers must invest in efficient payroll systems, stay informed about changing regulations, and prioritize compliance to ensure a smooth payroll process and maintain the trust of their employees while avoiding potential legal complications. Seeking professional advice from HR experts or payroll specialists can also be beneficial in navigating complex payroll-related matters.

FINANCIAL STATEMENTS AND MARKETING CAMPAIGN PHASES

"How to Interpret Financial Statements: A Guide for Managers

Financial statements can vary in complexity, ranging from detailed breakdowns to high-level summaries of a company's accounting. Understanding how to read and interpret these statements is crucial for effectively using the information they provide.

A financial statement is a document that records a company's financial activities, behaviors, and performance. It serves as a guide for analyzing business operations, refining strategies, and developing business plans. Accurate financial reporting is essential for maintaining compliance with government regulations, attracting investor support, and facilitating business transactions.

Financial statements contain different categories of information, depending on the purpose of each report. Various types of statements provide specific metrics for budgeting decisions, tracking incoming funds, and monitoring expenses.

Reading financial statements is important for anyone in the financial sector. Business owners and entrepreneurs need to possess a strong understanding of financial statements' significance. Even if financial responsibilities are outsourced to a director of finance or a team of accountants, being able to interpret a company's financial progress is essential for setting goals and implementing appropriate strategies.

There are several key types of financial statements that entrepreneurs should be familiar with.

Balance sheets, also known as statements of financial position, list a company's assets and how they contribute to the overall net worth of the business. These sheets include debts, liabilities, equipment, land, and other company possessions. By reading a balance sheet, one can gain insights into a company's ability to cover expenses and continue operations. Balance sheets often include summarized information from previous reporting periods, enabling a comparison of the business's growth and financial resources over time.

Business owners should regularly update their balance sheets to maintain an ongoing understanding of their company's value and financial obligations. Balance sheets categorize financial data into three types of accounts: assets, liabilities, and shareholder equity.

Assets refer to any cash, valuable goods, or products that belong to a business. They increase a company's value by reducing future expenses, generating revenue, or boosting sales. This category includes equipment, inventory, liquid cash, and intellectual property.

Liabilities represent debts owed by a company to other parties. They can include accounts payable, salaries, overdrafts, taxes, rent, utilities, and loans.

Equity, on a balance sheet, is the difference between assets and liabilities and encompasses the value of common stock, dividends paid to owners, and retained earnings. Retained earnings refer to the amount of revenue reinvested in the business for expenses and growth, instead of being distributed to shareholders.

When interpreting a balance sheet, it is important to calculate ratios for analyzing financial stability. Comparing the ratio of liabilities to assets provides insights into a company's value and performance. Having significantly more assets than liabilities indicate financial freedom and growth potential. Additional analysis methods include examining the debt-to-equity ratio, working capital, and quick ratio.

Cash flow statements provide an overview of a company's income and expenses over a specific period. These statements ensure that a business can cover short-term expenses and enable analysis of the sources of income. Typically, cash flow statements include three sections:

1. Operations: This section details how a company generates revenue and evaluates the profitability of its core services.

2. Investing: It highlights any outside investments and tracks return-on-investment over time.

3. Financing: Income from outside financing sources, dividends paid to stockholders, and company stock repurchases are included in this section.

Understanding a cash flow statement involves examining key numbers such as asset sales, income generated, and investments in company growth. Changes in overall cash flow compared to previous periods indicate a company's ability to break even using liquid assets. Additionally, attention should be given to how income is distributed across different departments and projects.

Income statements, or profit and loss statements, compare a company's overall gains and losses, including operating expenses and external factors. These statements incorporate information from cash flow statements and incorporate non-cash transactions like legal payouts, asset sales, and depreciation. Income statements are typically generated on a regular basis, such as monthly or quarterly.

Analyzing an income statement centers around the net income after tax, which investors and banks use to forecast a business's financial success. Evaluating which numbers contribute the most significant percentage to net income helps identify areas for expense reduction or investment in profitability.

Understanding and interpreting financial statements is a crucial skill for managers and business owners alike. By mastering this skill, one can make informed decisions, improve financial performance, and guide business strategies."

MARKETING CAMPAIGN PHASES

1. Formulate your objectives

The initial step of a marketing campaign involves clearly defining your objectives. This process determines the purpose behind your campaign and what you aim to accomplish. Your objectives can revolve around sales, customer satisfaction, the product itself, or another aspect.

It is crucial to ensure that your marketing campaign objectives align with your available resources. For instance, if your organization has recently acquired advanced email software, it would be unwise for your campaign objectives to primarily focus on social media engagement. By harmonizing your resources and objectives from the beginning, you will save employees' time and maintain projects within their designated budget.

Furthermore, bear in mind that your objectives primarily serve to measure the success of the campaign. As such, it is important for these objectives to be specific and measurable. For example, "increase sales" is a valuable objective, but it lacks specificity and does not provide clear guidance on how to achieve it.

Instead, enhance the specificity of the objective and establish a timeline to create something more definite, such as "sell 25 products per day." This objective is specific, time-driven, and measurable, making it easy to track the campaign's performance throughout its duration.

2. Establish your budget

Clearly outlining your campaign is crucial to its success. In addition to defining your campaign objectives, you must also determine a budget. This phase often goes hand-in-hand with setting campaign objectives, as these two steps feed off each other. The more ambitious and involved your objectives are, the higher your budget will need to be.

Just as the specific steps for creating a marketing campaign vary, there are several ways to develop a budget for the process. Your budget could be based on a percentage of revenue from current sales, derived from analyzing competitors' spending on similar marketing initiatives, or calculated by totaling the cost of tasks needed for the campaign. Regardless of the method you employ to establish your budget, it is important to clearly communicate it to the entire team and regularly monitor your spending to avoid exceeding it.

3. Define your target audience

The more accurately you can identify your target audience when launching your marketing campaign, the greater your return on investment will be. While having excellent objectives and the necessary budget are important, reaching the right audience is crucial to avoid falling short of your goals.

When defining your target audience, consider the following:

Demographic information, such as age, gender, and occupations.
Psychographic information, which reveals the attitudes, beliefs, and lifestyles of your audience.
Geographic location, as different locations have varying needs.

Industry, which may require adjusting marketing tactics to better target specific sectors.
Company size, as the needs of small and large companies differ significantly.
Preferred media channels, which can inform your marketing efforts by focusing on channels your audience already spends most of their time on.

The more information you can gather about your target audience, the better. This data enables you to customize your marketing campaign by delivering personalized messages that resonate with your audience.

4. Craft your message

One of the most crucial steps in a marketing campaign is developing an effective message. If you have conducted thorough research and clearly defined your target audience, creating a compelling campaign message becomes much easier.

Effective campaign messages address the following:

Tapping into the audience's emotions, highlighting unmet needs and pain points.
Emphasizing how the product can address those needs or pain points to benefit the audience.
Establishing your company as a credible expert.

Establishing credibility is the most challenging aspect of message development. Common methods for building trust with your audience include sharing customer testimonials, gathering endorsements from industry leaders, and publishing or referencing case studies that validate your claims.

5. Implement your campaign

Once you have laid out clear objectives, set a firm budget, and crafted your messaging, you are prepared to implement your campaign. This stage serves as your final opportunity to review your campaign and make any necessary adjustments before putting your plans into action.

Executing the campaign requires careful planning and coordination. Different departments will often handle various elements of the campaign, such as scheduling and marketing activities. For example, although you may have developed the overall campaign, another employee will be responsible for sending out campaign emails and ensuring they are scheduled in a manner that suits your audience.

During the campaign execution phase, your main challenge will be ensuring that each element of the campaign is disseminated correctly by the various departments involved, and that messaging is sent out at the appropriate time to the right people.

6. Evaluate your results

The final phase of a marketing campaign involves analyzing the results. This is where you determine whether your campaign successfully achieved the objectives you set and adhered to the budget. While most analysis occurs at the end of the campaign, it is also crucial to track and analyze metrics while the campaign is active.

In the analysis phase, it is important to utilize tools and platforms that help centralize your data and gather as much information as possible. Many media channels offer built-in metrics, such as click-through rates for emails, that can assist in evaluating the success of specific elements. However, one of the most valuable resources for analysis is a campaign management platform like Adobe Campaign.

A management platform enables you to plan your marketing campaign steps and track progress. It generates a dashboard that allows you to analyze the campaign comprehensively across multiple levels and channels, providing a consolidated view.

By thoroughly analyzing and reviewing your campaign results, you can identify areas where you met your objectives and determine key areas for growth and improvement. This analysis will enhance the success and effectiveness of future campaigns.

CHAPTER FOUR

BUSINESS-ENTITY SELECTION

There is currently a widespread discussion on social media regarding the formation of Limited Liability Companies (LLCs). Many individuals consider this option as a route to evading income tax payments or enrolling on an entrepreneurial career without knowledge of taxation and business operations. It deeply frustrates me when I am approached by clients who hold inaccurate information ahead of founding their own business, having oftentimes obtained such information through unreliable sources or individuals who are quick to offer advice yet lack any real expertise. It is *crucial* for aspiring entrepreneurs to understand that, when initiating a business, they *must* consult with lawyers, accountants, or financial advisors to acquire up-to-date advice surrounding the guidelines and legalities associated with this process. Both federal government and state authorities have established specific requirements that need to be adhered to. This is a primary motivation behind my decision to write this book. Within its pages, I aim to elucidate essential points and provide definitions pertaining to various types of business entities. Continuing our discussion so far, this chapter will address the selection criteria for different business entity types and shed light on the notion of self-employment tax on income received through your entrepreneurship.

AGENCY, PARTNERSHIP, AND LIMITED LIABILITY COMPANIES

Understanding the various types of agency relationships and the formation of business structures—like partnerships and limited liability companies—can be perplexing for the average person. Often, individuals unknowingly assume fiduciary duties[2] without fully comprehending their significance. When

[2] Fiduciary duties are legal and ethical obligations that one party owes to another when they are in a position of trust, confidence, and responsibility. Usually grounded in good faith, loyalty and a commitment to care, these

seeking employment, most people are focused on finding a job rather than considering the specific type of employment relationship they are entering, whether it be as an agent, employee, or subcontractor. The details of the employment arrangement often become apparent only after being hired, leading individuals to continue working out of necessity. Examples of agency relationships include roles such as insurance or real estate sales agents, where the principal is the insurance carrier or the realtor, respectively.

Additionally, many entrepreneurs venture into business with family or friends based on their innovative product or service ideas, often without understanding the concept of partnerships. Such a significant decision requires careful planning and education to ensure successful execution. The type of partnership chosen determines the liabilities borne by each partner. Unfortunately, some individuals enter business relationships without seeking guidance from legal or financial professionals.

Establishing a business can be a time-consuming and complex process, further complicated by the intricacies of business law. Small businesses, often run by individuals or families, are commonly set up as sole proprietorships due to their relatively straightforward nature. However, this may not always be the optimal choice for a particular business. Many business owners fail to seek proper assistance from accountants or lawyers, potentially exposing themselves to unnecessary risks. Without an appropriate business structure, owners may face direct liability if someone is injured on or near their premises.

DEFINITION OF AGENCY

An agency can be understood as a fiduciary relationship resulting from the mutual consent between two parties: the principal and the agent. The principal grants authority to the agent to act on their behalf, subject to their control. It is

---

duties require the party in the fiduciary role to act in the best interests of the other party, putting their interests ahead of their own.

important to note that the concept of agency extends beyond this basic definition. It encompasses a relationship established when the principal explicitly or implicitly authorizes the agent to act on their behalf. Both individuals and legal entities, such as partnerships or corporations, can assume the roles of principal or agent. Agency law, deeply rooted in contract law, governs these relationships. It is crucial for a principal to possess the contractual capacity to create an agency, which applies to general agencies.

Requirements for Principal and Agent

Regarding the requirements for a principal, mental capacity and a minimum age must be met to enter a contract. However, certain states allow minors to enter contracts for necessities like food, shelter, and clothing, despite their age. Such contracts by minors are generally voidable, except when they fall under the "necessaries clause," which prevents disaffirmation for vital needs. In the context of the entertainment industry, specific laws exist to protect minors from being taken advantage of in contracts that they might later want to nullify. On the other hand, the requirements for someone to be an agent are less restrictive and differ from those of a principal. Minimal mental capacity is sufficient to assume the role of an agent, if they can fulfill the obligations outlined in the agency contract. Unlike contracts that necessitate the exchange of money or benefits, creating an agency relationship does *not* require consideration from either party.

Types of Authority in an Agency Relationship

When forming an agency relationship, it is essential to consider the various types of authority that may arise. Three main types of authority exist: universal, general, and extraordinary. A universal agent possesses the power to engage in any activity on behalf of the principal. For example, a customer service representative has the authority to handle both simple and complex customer issues. In contrast, a general agent is authorized to engage in a series of transactions or all transactions of a specific type over a continuous period. Meanwhile, an extraordinary agent is granted limited authority to engage in a solitary or limited series of transactions for a fixed duration.

All three types of authority discussed above fall under the category of actual authority. Actual authority refers to the power that the principal delegates to the agent to act on their behalf. This authority can be expressly granted, either verbally or in writing. It can also be implied, resulting from the principal's conduct rather than an explicit statement. Implied authority can arise in several ways. Firstly, the agent may have the authority to take necessary or incidental actions to achieve the principal's objectives. Secondly, the agent may have the authority to act in accordance with industry customs and practices. Lastly, the agent may have the authority to continue any activity that the principal has previously consented to, even if the agent lacks explicit authorization.

Overall, it is crucial to understand the different types of authority that may arise in an agency relationship. Express and implied authority can both be granted, and any of the three types of actual authority may be present. Therefore, a careful evaluation of each type of authority is necessary to determine the extent of the agent's power to act on behalf of the principal.

Duties and Obligations of Agents and Principals

When establishing an agency relationship, the parties involved establish contractual obligations that the agent must fulfill. The agent must ensure that their actions adhere to the authorized terms of the agency agreement, as failure to do so constitute a breach of their responsibilities. In addition to contractual obligations, agents have a fiduciary duty of loyalty to the principal, requiring them to always act in the principal's best interest. This duty prohibits agents from engaging in self-dealing, representing adverse parties against the principal, or competing directly or indirectly with the principal. The agent must also respect the principal's confidential information and property, unless it is for the principal's benefit or with their informed consent. In certain cases, an agent may seek informed consent from the principal to engage in an otherwise prohibited behavior.

Agents are also expected to act reasonably, applying an objective standard of care, skill, and diligence like what another agent in a comparable circumstance would demonstrate. The specific knowledge and skills possessed by the agent may influence the expected level of care. Furthermore, agents have a duty of obedience, requiring them to carry out all lawful and reasonable instructions given by the principal. However, agents are *not* obligated to comply with illegal or unreasonable instructions. They must also behave reasonably to avoid causing harm to the principal. Additionally, agents have a duty of information sharing, which entails providing necessary information and maintaining proper records of the principal's assets.

Principals, meanwhile, must fulfill their obligations under the agency agreement and abide by the duties of good faith and fair dealing. This includes providing the agent with all required information and refraining from unduly interfering with the agent's assigned tasks. Besides, principals are responsible for compensating the agent and reimbursing any expenses incurred throughout the agency relationship. Failure to fulfill these obligations may result in legal actions, such as claims for contract or tort damages, requests for an accounting, or recovery of any prohibited gains.

In summary, agents have duties of loyalty, obedience, reasonable care, and information sharing, while principals must uphold their contractual obligations, act in good faith, and fulfill compensation duties. Breaching these obligations may lead to legal consequences, such as damages or accounting procedures, to address the issues that occurred.

Illustration of Agent's Duty and Principal's Responsibility

To provide you with a detailed illustration of an agent's duty and a principal's responsibility, I will refer to an ongoing arbitration case I have against a real estate office. In this case, I represent a buyer who engaged with the real estate office with an intention to purchase one of their listed properties. The seller agent represents the seller, who is considered the principal in this scenario. When the buyer approached my office and explained his case to me, I introduced them to the seller's agent to proceed with the purchase of a property listed by the agent. We entered the offer and counter phase, which is a part of contract law, and the buyer submitted an offer. Unfortunately, the seller elected to reject this offer. Communication ceased until several months later, when the seller's agent contacted my buyer and sold them the house *without* involving me. Consequently, I was not paid the commission that I had rightly earned due to all my earlier work with the buyer. In this situation, the seller's agent did not deal with me, a third party, in good faith.

LIABILITY OF A PRINCIPAL TO A THIRD PARTY

Let us commence by examining the circumstances wherein a principal *can* be held accountable for a contract entered with a third party. As previously discussed, actual authority refers to the power granted by a principal to an agent, allowing the agent to act on behalf of the principal. This authority can be explicitly granted by the principal, whether verbally or in writing, or it can be implied from the agent's actions or the surrounding circumstances. When an agent possessing actual authority enters a contract with a third party on behalf of the principal, the principal becomes legally obligated to the third party. This is stated in Restatement (Third) of Agency § 6.01.

Similarly, apparent authority arises when a principal presents the impression to a third party that an agent has the authority to act on behalf of the principal, even if the agent does not possess such power. In such situations, the principal's conduct can lead the third party to reasonably believe in the existence of an agency relationship. Consequently, the principal becomes liable to the third party for any contracts that the third party enters with the agent based on the agent's apparent authority. This too is outlined in Restatement (Third) of Agency § 6.01.

In the situation I described above, the seller's agent was granted actual authority by the principal, which means the authority was explicitly or implicitly given through written or verbal communication. This authority is evidenced by the note in the house listing, where the principal expressly allowed the agent to offer a commission to a buyer's agent. This written proof is crucial in demonstrating the agent's authority and my legitimate expectation of receiving the commission.

However, despite the clear grant of authority, the seller's agent did not act in good faith and continue respecting my role and responsibility in the process. Good faith is a fundamental principle in agency law, obligating agents to act honestly, fairly, and in the best interest of the principal. Unfortunately, the agent failed to fulfill this duty by not honoring the commitment to pay me the agreed commission. This breach of good faith puts the seller in a legally binding situation. As I seek to recover my commission, I have the option to pursue legal action against both the principal and the agent. The agent's actions directly affected the principal's legal position, making the principal ultimately responsible for any harm caused by the agent's breach of duty.

With the knowledge I have gained on this subject, I am confident in my ability to present a compelling case. I understand the legal principles surrounding agency authority, good faith, and the liability of principals for their agent's actions. Armed with this understanding, I can build a strong argument showcasing that the principal granted actual authority to the agent, the agent breached their duty of good faith, and I suffered a loss, therefore. Although my arbitration has been rescheduled, I remain optimistic about the outcome being in my favor. I believe that with the evidence and understanding I possess, I will effectively argue my case and rightfully recover the commission owed to me.

Additionally, many entrepreneurs venture into business with family or friends, typically having worked with them to devise a new product, yet many people fail to understand the concept of partnerships. Such a significant decision requires careful planning and education to ensure successful execution, and both parties should only enter an agreement when they fully understand what this entails. The type of partnership chosen determines the liabilities borne by each partner. Unfortunately, some individuals enter business relationships without seeking guidance from legal or financial professionals.

SOLE PROPRIETORSHIP

For individuals or couples embarking on the entrepreneurial journey, a sole proprietorship emerges as the most straightforward form of business structure. With this type of business, there is no need to undertake any formal procedures for establishment, and the business income is reported directly on the owner's personal tax return.

However, it is important to consider the potential drawbacks associated with a sole proprietorship. One significant disadvantage is that sole proprietors do not have legal separation from their businesses. Consequently, they assume personal liability for all the obligations and liabilities of the business. This means that in the unfortunate event of a lawsuit or financial claims against the business, the sole proprietor's personal assets, including their bank accounts, residence, and vehicles, could be at risk.

It is crucial to note that a sole proprietorship is most suitable for businesses that are owned and operated by an individual or a couple and do not involve the employment of additional staff members or engage in significant contractual agreements with landlords, vendors, suppliers, or subcontractors. By keeping the business operations simple and limited to the owner's direct involvement, the risks and complexities associated with managing employees and extensive external relationships can be minimized. Since this route may be the most preferred amongst the readers of this book, I explicitly list the benefits of sole proprietorship below:

- ✓ **Easy and inexpensive formation:** Establishing a sole proprietorship is relatively simple and inexpensive compared to other business structures. It typically involves minimal paperwork and legal formalities, making it a popular choice for entrepreneurs and small businesses.
- ✓ **Complete control:** As the sole owner, you have full control over all aspects of the business. You can make decisions independently without having to consult with partners or shareholders. This allows for quick decision-making and flexibility in adapting to changing market conditions.
- ✓ **Direct ownership of profits:** All profits generated by the business belong solely to the owner. There is no need to share profits with partners or shareholders, which can be a significant advantage for individuals seeking to maximize their personal income.

- ✓ **Tax flexibility:** A sole proprietorship offers tax flexibility. The business itself is not taxed separately from the owner. Instead, the owner reports business income and expenses on their personal tax return. This can simplify the tax filing process and potentially result in lower tax obligations than other business structures.
- ✓ **Minimal regulatory requirements:** Unlike corporations or partnerships, sole proprietorships are subject to fewer regulatory requirements. There are typically fewer reporting and compliance obligations, reducing administrative burdens and costs.
- ✓ **Confidentiality:** Sole proprietorships offer privacy and confidentiality. Since there are no partners or shareholders, financial and operational information about the business generally remains private. This can be advantageous for individuals who prefer to keep their business affairs confidential.
- ✓ **Easy dissolution:** If you decide to close the business, it is generally straightforward to dissolve a sole proprietorship. There are usually no complicated legal processes or formalities involved, making it easier to exit the business when desired.

GENERAL PARTNERSHIP

When two or more business owners come together to conduct business activities without establishing a separate legal entity, their arrangement is automatically classified as a general partnership. In such a partnership, the responsibilities and decision-making authority are typically shared among the partners, as are the profits and losses generated by the business.

Like a sole proprietorship, however, a general partnership does not provide any form of protection to its partners against liability for the obligations and debts incurred by the business. As such, partners' personal assets can be at risk if the business fails to fulfill its financial obligations or faces legal claims. For this reason, general partnerships are often advised against by legal professionals. legal professionals often caution against operating as a general partnership. This is exacerbated by an additional issue in which general partnerships are typically not formalized with a legally binding agreement.

Indeed, many partners neglect to sign a formal agreement outlining the terms and conditions of their partnership, including profit distribution, decision-making processes, and dispute resolution mechanisms. This oversight can create significant problems and costly disputes down the line, as the absence of a clear agreement can result in misunderstandings, disagreements, and potential legal battles.

What should emerge from this brief description is that any individuals seeking to engage in a general partnership ought to carefully consider alternative business structures that provide limited liability protection. By establishing a formal legal structure and drafting a comprehensive partnership agreement, partners can define their roles, responsibilities, and protections, thereby minimizing the risk of costly conflicts and personal financial losses.

Being in a partnership with a family member taught me a valuable lesson; not everyone should enter a business relationship together. When embarking on this venture, I held the belief that each of us would play an active role in the management of the business, contribute financially on an equal basis, and share a mutual desire for the success and growth of our enterprise.

However, reality proved to be far different from my expectations. Rather than working together to make important decisions, I found myself solely responsible for bearing the weight of such choices. From shoveling the snow to responding to emergency phone calls, it was apparent that the burden fell solely on my shoulders. Most frustratingly, my efforts to push the company forward and achieve progress were met with resistance from my business partner.

Although we would engage in discussions about ways to propel the company forward, any decision to advance would be met with pushback. Nonetheless, I persevered and made decisions for the betterment and advancement of the business. Curiously, my partner would then falsely claim agreement with these decisions, even though he had never supported them.

Through this experience, I learned the significance of selecting the right business partner. The realization dawned upon me that not everyone possesses the dedication, drive, and willingness to work harmoniously towards shared goals. It is crucial to carefully consider such factors before entering a business partnership, especially with a family member.

In conclusion, my partnership with a family member served as a valuable lesson. It underscored that while the notion of collaboration and shared goals may be appealing, it is essential to ensure that everyone involved possesses the attributes necessary for success. A business partnership demands mutual dedication, clear communication, and aligned visions. Failure to recognize these critical aspects can hinder the progress and prosperity of the company.

VENTURE PARTNERSHIP

Venture partnerships refer to collaborative agreements between two or more entities, typically businesses or investors, who join forces to pursue a specific business opportunity or venture. These partnerships are formed with the aim of harnessing the complementary skill sets, resources, and expertise of the partners to achieve common goals and increase the chances of success.

One of the key advantages of venture partnerships is the pooling of resources. Each partner brings their own set of assets, such as capital, technology, networks, or market access, which can significantly enhance the overall capabilities of the venture. By combining these resources, partners can overcome individual limitations, tap into new markets, or develop innovative products or services that would have been challenging to achieve independently.

Moreover, venture partnerships promote knowledge sharing and experiential learning. The diverse backgrounds and perspectives of the partners lead to a cross-pollination of ideas and best practices, fostering an environment of creativity and innovation. Partners may have different industry expertise or geographic reach, allowing for the exploration of new markets or the application of existing capabilities in different contexts. Venture partnerships also mitigate risks by spreading them across multiple entities. When partners share the burden of financial, operational, and market risks, they can collectively navigate challenges and sustain the venture during difficult times. Furthermore, partnerships can provide access to a wider customer base or distribution channels, enabling faster market penetration and increased potential for revenue generation.

In conclusion, venture partnerships enable businesses and investors to collaborate effectively, combining their resources and expertise to pursue mutually beneficial opportunities. By leveraging these partnerships, organizations can accelerate innovation, mitigate risks, and expand their market reach, leading to enhanced competitiveness and successful ventures.

Venture partnerships differ from other types of business partnerships in several ways:

1. Focus on high-growth opportunities: Venture partnerships are specifically formed to pursue high-growth opportunities and invest in companies or projects with high potential for significant returns. These partnerships typically focus on startups or early-stage companies operating in innovative and emerging industries.

2. Risk and return: Venture partnerships involve higher levels of risk compared to other partnerships. They invest in high-risk ventures, such as technology, biotech, or other industries with uncertain prospects. In return, venture partnerships seek high returns on investment if the ventures succeed.

3. Strategic nature: Venture partnerships often involve strategic alliances between different parties to combine their expertise, resources, and networks in pursuit of a common goal. These partnerships can involve venture capitalists, angel investors, corporations, or other entities that bring complementary skills or resources to the table.

4. Shorter-term duration: Venture partnerships are often focused on achieving specific objectives within a relatively shorter time frame compared to other partnerships. They may have a specific investment horizon or exit strategy in mind, such as an IPO, acquisition, or other liquidity event.

5. Active involvement: Venture partnerships often provide active management or advisory support to the companies they invest in. They may take board seats, provide mentorship, and actively participate in the decision-making processes of the ventures they back, aiming to enhance their chances of success.

6. Specialized knowledge: Venture partnerships typically require specialized knowledge and expertise in evaluating high-growth ventures, emerging markets, or disruptive technologies. The partners involved may have a deep understanding of specific industries, market trends, or technological advancements, allowing them to make informed investment decisions.

7. Fund structure: Venture partnerships are often structured as investment funds, such as venture capital funds or private equity funds. Limited partners provide the capital to the partnership, and a general partner or fund

manager is responsible for making investment decisions and managing the fund's operations.

Overall, venture partnerships differentiate themselves from other forms of business partnerships by focusing on high-growth opportunities, taking higher risks for potentially higher returns, forming strategic alliances, and actively participating in the ventures they invest in.

Forming and maintaining venture partnerships come with their own set of unique challenges and benefits compared to other forms of business partnerships. Here are some of them:

Challenges:
1. Shared Risk: Venture partnerships often involve high-risk endeavors, such as launching new products or entering new markets. The challenge lies in managing and sharing this risk between partners effectively.
2. Alignment of Goals: It can be difficult to align the long-term goals and objectives of various venture partners. Each partner may have different strategies or priorities, which may lead to conflicts or disagreements.
3. Decision-making: With multiple partners involved, decision-making can become challenging. Balancing different perspectives and priorities may slow down the decision-making process and hinder the ability to respond swiftly to market changes.
4. Differences in Culture and Management Style: Venture partnerships may involve partners from different backgrounds, cultures, or industries. These differences can create challenges in communication, collaboration, and managing expectations.
5. Exit Strategy: Unlike other forms of business partnerships, venture partnerships often have an exit strategy in mind. Determining when and how to exit the partnership can be complex, especially if partners have different timelines or expectations.

Benefits:

1. Access to Resources: Venture partnerships can provide access to a wider range of resources, including expertise, technology, networks, and funding. This can help accelerate growth and increase competitiveness in the market.
2. Risk-sharing and Cost-sharing: Venture partnerships allow partners to share the financial burden and risk associated with new ventures. Pooling resources and costs can make it more feasible to undertake ambitious projects or enter new markets.
3. Complementary Skill Sets: Partnering with individuals or organizations possessing different skills and knowledge can bring valuable expertise to the table. This diversity can enhance problem-solving, innovation, and overall business performance.
4. Increased Market Reach: By collaborating with established partners, ventures can access new markets, customers, or distribution channels. This can create opportunities for expansion and market penetration.
5. Learning and Growth: Venture partnerships often foster a culture of learning and knowledge exchange. Partners can gain insights, perspectives, and best practices from each other, leading to personal and professional growth.

Ultimately, venture partnerships can offer unique benefits, such as access to resources and shared risk, but also present challenges in aligning goals, decision-making, and managing differences. Choosing the right partners and maintaining effective communication and collaboration are crucial for the success of such partnerships.

LIMITED PARTNERSHIP

A limited partnership is a legal structure that consists of two tiers of partners—at least one general partner and at least one limited partner—each with distinct roles and responsibilities. It provides a flexible framework for businesses that seek to combine the benefits of active management and limited liability.

In a limited partnership, the general partner assumes an active role in operating the business and takes on personal liability for any obligations and debts incurred over the course of the partnership. As such, they hold complete authority for the decisions and day-to-day operations of the corporation. The limited partner's primary role, by contrast, is to contribute capital without directly participating in management of the business. The limited partner enjoys the benefit of sharing in the profits generated by the partnership, which are typically calculated proportionally to their investment. Importantly, the limited partner's liability is limited to the extent of their investment, meaning that all personal assets are protected from the partnership's debts beyond their initial contribution.

Limited partnerships are particularly attractive to businesses that require outside investors or passive contributors who do not wish to be involved in the day-to-day operations. Examples may be start-ups requiring funds for product development or marketing. These investors can provide financial resources without taking on the risks and responsibilities of active management. Limited partnerships are commonly found in industries such as real estate, venture capital, and private equity, where there exists a need for capital infusion and expertise from different parties. However, it is worth noting that many businesses have recently opted for alternative legal structures, such as the limited liability company (LLC; see later in the chapter). An LLC offers similar benefits to a limited partnership, including limited liability protection for all members.

In summary, a limited partnership is a legal entity that accommodates the involvement of both active managers, known as general partners, and passive investors, known as limited partners. It allows for the sharing of profits while limiting the liability of the limited partners. However, with the rise of the LLC structure, many businesses now choose the LLC as it combines the advantages of limited liability with a more adaptable management structure.

LIMITED LIABILITY PARTNERSHIP

The limited liability partnership (LLP) stands as a legal structure that shares structural similarities with a general partnership (and a very similar name to a limited partnership!) while offering partners an additional layer of protection from personal liability. LLPs have gained prominence in recent years, particularly among professionals such as lawyers, architects and accountants, who seek to safeguard themselves from potential financial repercussions arising from their work or the malpractice of their fellow partners. It is worth noting that regulations in certain states prohibit these professionals from establishing corporations or limited liability companies (LLCs), making the LLP an attractive alternative.

In essence, LLP operates as a hybrid entity that combines features from both partnerships and corporations, bestowing distinct advantages upon its partners. Like a general partnership, an LLP fosters collaboration among partners who jointly undertake business activities, contributing their skills, expertise, and resources to achieve common objectives. However, the defining characteristic of an LLP lies in the liability protection it provides to its partners.

In a traditional general partnership, the partners assume unlimited personal liability for the debts, obligations, and liabilities incurred by the business. This implies that if one partner is unable to fulfill their financial obligations, the remaining partners become individually responsible for covering those liabilities. The fundamental principle of the LLP is to alleviate this burden by limiting partners' personal liability for the actions, debts, and malpractice of their fellow partners.

This limited liability shield in an LLP shields partners from being held personally liable for the professional negligence or malpractice committed by their partners. This means that if a partner engages in professional misconduct or commits an error leading to financial losses or legal claims, the personal assets of the other partners remain protected, safeguarding them from potential financial ruin. Each partner is accountable for their own actions and professional conduct, while being insulated from the consequences of the actions of other partners within the LLP. This may be especially attractive if you are entering into business with individuals that you do not know well on a personal level.

The establishment and operation of an LLP are governed by specific laws and regulations, which may vary across jurisdictions. To form an LLP, partners typically file the necessary documents with the appropriate government agency, providing information about the partnership's structure, partners' roles and responsibilities, and the nature of the business. Some states may require LLPs to register and maintain additional records or meet certain professional licensing requirements to ensure ethical practice within their respective fields.

In summary, a limited liability partnership (LLP) offers a valuable legal structure for professionals who desire to collaborate with partners while safeguarding themselves from personal liability for the actions or malpractice of their fellow partners. LLPs combine the advantages of partnerships with the added benefit of limited personal liability, shielding partners' assets from potential financial harm. As regulations and requirements may differ across jurisdictions, it is important to consult legal and professional advisors when considering the formation of an LLP.

LIMITED LIABILITY COMPANY

An LLC, or Limited Liability Company, is a business structure that offers a level of protection to its owners, who are referred to as "members." As with LLPs, the fundamental advantage of an LLC lies in its ability to shield members from personal liability for the company's debts and obligations. This means that if the LLC is unable to fulfill its financial obligations or faces legal action, only the assets owned by the business are at risk, while the members' personal assets are generally safeguarded. It is important to note, however, that members are still responsible for their individual acts of negligence or misconduct.

A significant advantage inherent to the LLC structure resides in its notable taxation flexibility. This organizational form possesses the capacity to assume the characteristics of a sole proprietorship or a partnership for taxation considerations, enabling the disclosure of gains and losses within the confines of the members' personal tax filings. Conversely, an LLC may elect for corporate taxation, a strategic choice that could offer distinct benefits under specific circumstances. This flexibility, not possible in most other business structures, provides members with the opportunity to select the tax structure that best suits their business needs. The management structure of an LLC is highly adaptable; it can be managed directly by its members or may opt to appoint designated managers who are responsible for managing the company. This versatility allows for different management styles and ensures that the LLC can be tailored to the preferences and expertise of its members.

Additionally, an LLC can have a single member or multiple members, rendering it an attractive option for businesses of all sizes and types, from small family-owned enterprises to larger partnerships. Another advantage of forming an LLC is the reduced burden of record keeping, meetings, and reporting requirements compared to corporations. Indeed, LLCs generally have fewer formalities and administrative obligations, making it easier for members to focus on running their businesses without being overwhelmed by extensive paperwork and compliance measures.

It's tempting to consider LLC as objectively the best choice for your venture. However, there are certain situations where an LLC may *not* be the most suitable choice, and it is important that you understand these fully. For instance, if your business plans involve seeking venture capital or angel investors, or if you have ambitions of taking your company public, forming an LLC may not align with these objectives. Furthermore, it is worth noting that LLCs are a relatively recent addition to the business landscape, and as a result, there is generally less formal guidance and legal precedent available for LLCs compared to corporations (see below). While LLCs are widely recognized and accepted, the body of law surrounding them may not be as extensive or well-established. Therefore, it is important for LLC owners to seek professional advice and guidance to ensure compliance with applicable laws and regulations.

In short, an LLC provides members flexibility and limited liability. It offers tax choices, varied management, and suits diverse ownership. It's low administrative load benefits small businesses, but complex goals like VC, IPO, or clear legal structure may favor other structures.

CORPORATION

When it comes to shielding owners, known as "shareholders," from personal liability, corporations stand on equal footing with LLCs. By establishing a corporation, individuals can protect their personal assets from the potential debts and legal obligations of the business. Nevertheless, it is worth noting that corporations typically involve slightly more intricate record keeping and reporting requirements, which may vary depending on the specific state in which the incorporation takes place.

Corporations can be categorized into two main types: "C corporations" and "S corporations." A C corporation is subject to corporate income tax, which means that the company's profits are taxed separately from its shareholders. Additionally, the shareholders of a C corporation are obligated to pay taxes on the dividends and income they receive from the corporation. On the other hand, S corporations are not subjected to corporate-level taxation. Instead, the business income flows through to the shareholders' personal tax returns, avoiding the double taxation typically associated with C corporations. For entrepreneurs seeking guidance on the most suitable tax status for their specific business circumstances, consulting an accountant or tax advisor is highly recommended.

In terms of ownership and transferability, corporations offer a distinct advantage. The shares of a corporation can be easily transferred from one individual to another. This feature proves particularly valuable when aiming to attract external financial support or distribute ownership among employees or individuals who have contributed to the startup's growth. The ability to transfer shares effortlessly enhances the marketability and liquidity of corporate ownership, making it an appealing option for many outside investors seeking investment opportunities.

Put simply, corporations offer liability protection like LLCs but add record keeping complexities. C vs. S corporations yield varied tax outcomes for corps and shareholders, and it is essential that you seek expert tax advice before making decisions regarding your ideal tax status.

NONPROFIT CORPORATION

If your primary objective is to make a positive impact on society or support a noble cause rather than solely pursuing financial gains for the owners, establishing a nonprofit corporation may be the ideal choice for your business. Nonprofit corporations offer the same level of liability protection as their for-profit counterparts, ensuring that the personal assets of the owners remain separate from the organization's liabilities.

Once you have successfully formed a nonprofit corporation in accordance with the regulations of your state, it is crucial to seek tax-exempt status from the Internal Revenue Service (IRS). This tax-exempt status is essential to avail certain benefits and exemptions that can significantly contribute to the financial sustainability of your nonprofit. To qualify for tax-exempt status, you are required to meet specific criteria established by the IRS.

One of the fundamental requirements for tax-exempt status is that any profits generated by the nonprofit must be utilized for managing and furthering the goals of the organization or the charitable cause it supports. Unlike for-profit corporations, nonprofit organizations are not permitted to distribute dividends or profits to shareholders or owners. Instead, these funds should be reinvested in the organization's activities, programs, and initiatives to fulfill its mission and make a positive difference in the community or the target beneficiaries.

By adhering to these guidelines, nonprofit corporations can demonstrate their commitment to serving the public good and can potentially benefit from tax advantages, such as exemption from federal income taxes and the ability to receive tax-deductible contributions from donors. These tax benefits, coupled with the ability to access grants and funding opportunities specifically available to nonprofit entities, can provide crucial support for the sustainability and growth of your organization.

It is important to note that maintaining tax-exempt status requires ongoing compliance with IRS regulations and reporting requirements. Nonprofits must carefully track and document their financial activities, maintain transparency and accountability, and file annual information returns, such as the IRS Form 990, to provide an overview of their operations and financial status. By establishing a nonprofit corporation and obtaining tax-exempt status, you can position your organization as a credible and dedicated entity focused on making a meaningful impact in society. This legal structure not only provides liability protection but also opens doors to various resources, partnerships, and funding opportunities that can fuel the growth and effectiveness of your nonprofit's mission.

CHOOSING A BUSINESS STRUCTURE

When faced with the decision of selecting a legal structure for your new business, particularly if it could potentially fit into multiple categories, determining the most appropriate option is not always a straightforward task. To assist you in making an informed decision, I recommend that you consider the following areas. I wish to also use this time to remind you that you can seek guidance from a certified public accountant (CPA) for personalized insights based on your unique situation.

Flexibility

The trajectory and destination of your company lie at the forefront of our strategic planning. To determine the optimal legal structure that facilitates your envisioned growth, you should refer to your business plan, ensuring alignment between your objectives and the chosen entity. The goal should always be to adopt a legal structure that not only accommodates growth but also embraces the potential for transformation, unhindered by unnecessary constraints. When crafting your business plan, carefully outline your short-term and long-term goals, considering various aspects such as market trends, customer demands, competitive landscapes, and technological advancements. By gaining a comprehensive understanding of your objectives, you will be well-positioned to effectively evaluate which legal structure is most conducive to your growth trajectory. This strategic decision ensures that we can seize emerging opportunities, adapt to market dynamics, attract capital investment, and foster an environment that inspires innovation and success.

Complexity

When delving into the realm of startup ventures and operational intricacies, one business structure stands out for its simplicity: the sole proprietorship. Establishing a sole proprietorship is a relatively straightforward process that involves registering one's name, commencing business activities, and subsequently reporting the generated profits as personal income while fulfilling tax obligations. While this form of business ownership offers a streamlined approach, it may pose challenges when it comes to securing external funding. Partnerships require a carefully crafted agreement to define roles and profit sharing, whereas corporations and LLCs introduce a higher level of complexity with various reporting obligations. Each business structure comes with its own set of advantages and considerations, and entrepreneurs must weigh the pros and cons to determine the most suitable path for their specific goals and circumstances and consider this against the complexity they are willing to undertake.

Liability

In the realm of personal liability, corporations stand out as entities that provide the least exposure to personal assets. The law recognizes corporations as separate legal entities, distinct from their officers and shareholders.

Consequently, in the event of lawsuits initiated by creditors or customers, the law prohibits them from gaining access to the personal assets of these officers or shareholders. LLCs also offer a comparable level of personal liability protection while offering the added tax benefits typically associated with sole proprietorships. On the other hand, partnerships present a different structure, with liability shared among the partners as dictated by the terms established in their partnership agreement. Unlike corporations and LLCs, it is crucial you understand that partners in a partnership can potentially be held personally liable for the actions or debts of the partnership. The extent of this liability is determined by the specific terms outlined in the partnership agreement, highlighting the importance of careful drafting and negotiation when forming any such contract.

Taxes

An owner of an LLC follows a similar tax structure to that of a sole proprietor. All profits generated by the LLC are considered personal income and are subject to taxation at the end of the year, ensuring that the owner is not taxed separately as a company but rather as an individual. By avoiding double taxation, which occurs when both the business entity and the owner are taxed separately, the LLC structure provides a favorable tax treatment for small business owners, particularly in the early stages of their business.

Jennifer Friedman, a principal at River, emphasizes the importance of avoiding double taxation in the early stages of a small business. By choosing the LLC structure, small business owners can ensure that their profits are not subject to corporate-level taxation but are instead treated as personal income. In the case of a partnership, each partner also claims their share of the profits as personal income. It is common for partners to consult their accountants, who may recommend making quarterly or biannual advance tax payment to minimize the impact of the tax liability on their annual tax return. Finally, corporations operate under a different tax structure. It files its own tax returns annually, reporting its profits after deducting expenses, including payroll costs. The corporation is subject to corporate-level taxes on its profits. However, when the corporation pays its owner(s), they are required to pay personal taxes (which may include Social Security and Medicate payments) on the income they receive.

HOW TO SET-UP AN ENTITY: A SUMMARY

Setting up an entity, whether it's a business or a non-profit organization, can be an exciting venture, but it requires careful planning and execution. Considering the abundance of information, we have looked at over the course of this chapter, I have created a step-by-step guide that can help you navigate this often-daunting process and set up your entity successfully.

1. Define Your Purpose and Goals

Before diving into the legalities, take the time to define the purpose and goals of your entity. Whether you're starting a business to offer a new product or service or establishing a non-profit organization to address a particular social issue, having a clear vision is crucial. Understand the problem you aim to solve or the value you want to provide. This clarity will serve as the foundation for your entity and guide your decisions throughout the setup process.

2. Choose the Right Legal Structure

Selecting the appropriate legal structure is essential for your entity's success. Each structure comes with its own set of benefits and drawbacks, affecting aspects such as taxation, liability, and management. Common options include sole proprietorship, partnership, corporation, LLC, and non-profit organization. Consider the nature of your entity, your long-term goals, and the level of control you desire before deciding.

3. Register Your Entity

Once you've determined the legal structure, it's time to register your entity with the relevant government authorities. This step involves completing the necessary paperwork, providing essential information about your entity, and paying any required fees. Depending on your country and the type of entity, you might need to register with the local, state, or federal government. Make sure to check for any additional permits or licenses specific to your industry.

4. Obtain an EIN and Set Up Banking

An Employer Identification Number (EIN) is a unique identifier required for tax purposes and other financial transactions. You can obtain an EIN from the tax authority in your country, such as the Internal Revenue Service (IRS) in the United States. After acquiring the EIN, open a separate bank account for your entity to keep personal and business finances distinct. Having a dedicated bank account ensures clarity in financial matters and simplifies accounting.

5. Comply with Legal and Regulatory Requirements

Ensure your entity complies with all legal and regulatory requirements in your jurisdiction. This includes understanding tax obligations, labor laws, zoning regulations, and any industry-specific rules. Failure to comply with these laws can lead to severe consequences for your entity, such as fines or legal disputes. Consider seeking professional advice from attorneys, accountants, or business advisors to ensure you are on the right track.

Setting up an entity can be a rewarding experience when approached with careful planning and adherence to legal guidelines. Take the time to define your entity's purpose, choose the appropriate legal structure, and register it with the relevant authorities. Obtain the necessary EIN and set up a dedicated bank account to manage your entity's finances effectively. Finally, prioritize compliance with all applicable laws and regulations to build a solid foundation for your entity's growth and success. With a well-thought-out approach, your entity will be on the path to accomplishing its goals and making a positive impact.

CHAPTER FIVE

BUSINESS LOANS

As I reflect on the concept of borrowing, a popular Hip Hop song—*OPP* by Naughty by Nature—comes to mind. Besides its insatiably catchy tune, the lyrical content resonates closely with my generation, embodying the idea of using other people's assets. Following this theme, let us explore the notion of being "down with other people's money." Just like the banking system, we as individuals thrive on borrowing funds. When we deposit our money into the bank, we earn minimal interest income while the bank takes our funds and lends them to others. This, if you have ever wondered, is how your bank generates its profits. And it’s a lucrative business. Still, the symbiotic relationship of utilizing other people's money is one that many of us benefit from, too. Consider credit cards, for example. They enable us to make purchases with borrowed funds. We all enjoy using other people's resources, be it money or material possessions.

Financial planners often caution against borrowing money, but I encourage you to keep an open mind. After all, there should be no one-size-fits-all rule when it comes to this topic. Instead of dismissing their advice entirely, then, let's begin by reframing it. Borrowing money may not be suitable for everyone, but perhaps we ought to consider why we want to borrow money in the first place. Even in the realm of investments, such as stocks and bonds, we leverage borrowed funds through margin loan programs to amplify our potential profits. In many cases, this is a perfectly valid (though not guaranteed) route to boosting your income. Furthermore, borrowing money can be an effective means to kickstart your business endeavors. Many of the most famous companies today would never have gotten off the ground if their founders followed the advice to never borrow money. So, let’s look at it more sensibly. Are you ready to embrace other people's money? We're all familiar with the concept and borrowing funds can serve as a catalyst for various opportunities. By understanding the nuances of borrowing wisely, we can leverage these financial tools to our advantage.

How To Get a Business Loan In 5 Steps

These 5 steps how to get a business loan by Jerry Brown that I found on Forbes advisor was well instructed. One should follow those guidelines in how to go about obtaining a business loan.

A business loan enables the acquisition of necessary funds to grow business activities, meet daily expenditures, and procure equipment or inventory. If you lack experience in applying for a business loan, you may be uncertain about the initial steps and necessary documentation. Thus, presented is a straightforward guide that will assist you in examining your options and efficiently assembling your business loan application in five accessible stages.

1. Determine the Purpose of Financing
There are various types of small business loans available, so it is important to identify the specific reason for needing financing. This will help in selecting the most suitable loan option. Here are a few common scenarios:

- Acquiring new equipment: Some lenders offer equipment loans designed to assist in purchasing machinery or office furniture. These loans are secured by the equipment itself, giving the lender the right to seize it if the loan is not repaid.
- Borrowing a small amount of money: To borrow a small sum, consider applying for a microloan. The U.S. Small Business Administration (SBA) provides a Microloan program that allows qualified applicants to borrow up to $50,000. Other organizations, such as Kiva and the Women's Microfinance Initiative, also offer microloans.
- Establishing a business: Startup loans for new businesses can be challenging to obtain due to minimum time in business requirements imposed by most lenders. In such cases, applying for a microloan or a business credit card could be an option. Business credit cards may be easier to qualify for as they are based on personal credit scores.
- Covering day-to-day operations: A working capital loan can help in dealing

with temporary cash flow problems by providing short-term funding for daily expenses like payroll and rent.
- Borrowing funds as needed: For those uncertain about the exact amount needed to borrow, a business line of credit may be suitable. Once approved, funds can be withdrawn up to a predetermined amount, and interest is only charged on the borrowed sum.

2. Assess Eligibility for a Business Loan
Although requirements for business loans vary among lenders, here are four factors commonly considered during the evaluation of a small business loan application:

- Credit score: Lenders assess personal and business credit scores to evaluate the likelihood of loan repayment. Higher credit scores generally increase the chances of loan approval and result in lower interest rates.
- Collateral and personal guarantee: Some lenders require collateral, an asset of value that can be seized if the loan defaults. A personal guarantee may also be necessary, securing the loan with personal assets such as savings, a home, or other valuables.
- Time in business: Traditional banks typically require a minimum of two years of business operation, while online lenders may accept one year. Certain online lenders even consider applicants with only six months of business history.
- Annual revenue: Total annual sales also play a significant role. It is important to review business finances and check with the lender to ensure eligibility requirements are met.

3. Compare Different Business Lending Options
There are several avenues to explore when seeking a small business loan. The three most common types of lenders are:

- Online lenders: Online lenders offer a range of loan products, including term loans, merchant cash advances, lines of credit, and microloans. Approval rates for online lenders were higher than traditional banks in 2019, partly due to their less stringent requirements. However, it's worth noting that online lenders often charge higher interest rates.

- Traditional banks: Traditional banks provide similar loan types as online lenders. One advantage of applying with a bank is the potential for lower rates, especially for well-qualified applicants. However, they usually have stricter eligibility criteria. Additionally, obtaining funds from traditional banks can take longer, leading to delays.

- Microlenders: Microlenders are nonprofit organizations that offer microloans up to $50,000, catering to small business owners who do not qualify for traditional business loans. Microlenders typically have more lenient eligibility requirements compared to banks. For instance, Kiva approves applicants based on "social capital" rather than credit scores.

4. Compile the Required Documents
Once the ideal lending option is identified, gather the necessary documents. Lenders often request the following items:

- Personal and business tax returns
- Business licenses
- Articles of incorporation
- Personal and business bank statements
- Profit and loss statements
- Financial statements
- Business plan
- Building lease

If unsure about the specific documents required, it is advisable to contact the lender before submitting an application.

The final step in the process is to submit your small business loan application. Depending on the chosen lender, this can be done either online or in person. The lender will require certain information such as your name, business name, Social Security number (SSN), desired loan amount, loan purpose, Business Tax ID, and annual revenue. Once the application is submitted, you'll need to wait for an approval decision. If the loan is approved, the lender will send you a loan agreement to sign before providing the funds or a line of credit. When selecting the best business loan, it is important to compare the loans you qualify for and determine which one fits your needs. Factors to consider include the annual percentage rate (APR), fees, repayment terms, and funding speed. Getting a business loan from a bank can involve either an online application or visiting a branch, with information such as business name, start date, gross annual revenue, and annual household income for all owners being required. Banks often have stricter eligibility requirements, so a strong credit history and financials may be necessary to qualify.

History of Global Financial System

Over recent decades, the global financial system has garnered a reputation as a supposed root cause of countless world problems. However, it is important to recognize that finance was initially designed to enhance our quality of life and streamline business operations. It was never created with a purpose to cause us grief! Indeed, the planned benefits are still very much accessible; a well-functioning financial system offers numerous advantages, such as enabling us to purchase essential goods for comfortable living and facilitating connections between those in need of funds and potential lenders. Additionally, it supports the insurance industry, allowing us to protect ourselves from unforeseen disasters and secure our assets for future generations. Without the comfort blanket of insurance, starting your own business would be infinitely more stressful and riskier.

Among the mutually beneficial aspects of finance are mortgages, empowering individuals to become property owners by obtaining loans and making regular payments with interest to lenders. On a larger scale, a robust financial system can positively influence society, as is evident from the progress made over recent centuries. The strong financial sectors of countries like Great Britain and the Netherlands were unmistakably instrumental in their meteoric rise to global power during the early years of industrialization. In a similar vein, substantial investments in developing nations today are made possible by strong finances, leading to an improved standard of living for the population.

On the other end of the spectrum, we can observe the failures of dictator-driven financial systems in communist countries, where central control hinders the flow of money to businesses in need, resulting in limited job opportunities and weakened economic growth. While capitalist freedom has driven prosperous industrialization, contributing significantly to modern society, not all financial innovations stemming from this system have been beneficial. In fact, some have had notably adverse effects on people's lives. It emerges; therefore, the financial industry has at times lost sight of its initial purpose: to aid the wellbeing of our global population. It is evident that the financial industry has at times, lost sight of its impact on the global population's well-being. The following book summaries will delve into the reasons behind this phenomenon, exploring both positive and negative aspects of financial innovations.

Discover the key ideas from John Kay's book, "Other People's Money," which delves into the prevalence of financial crises and their impact on society. The book aims to demystify the complexity of the financial sector and shed light on the reasons behind the 2008 financial crisis. By reading this summary, you'll gain insights into why the financial sector holds immense significance while also posing significant risks.

THE VITALITY OF FINANCE

Finance is undeniably one of the foundational facets upholding modern society. Its necessity lies in its power to facilitate economic activities, allocate resources efficiently, and support innovation and growth. This complex, ever-evolving system is a fundamental shaper of the dynamic global economy, influencing the daily lives and operations of individuals, businesses, and governments alike. Below, we explore some of the key reasons why finance is so vital and why its efficient functioning is crucial for the well-being of society.

- **Resource Allocation:** Finance facilitates the allocation of resources across various sectors and industries. Capital flows and investment decisions determine which projects receive funding and which do not. By ensuring that scarce resources are directed to the most productive and promising ventures, finance can thus promote economic growth and job creation.
- **Risk Management:** In a world of uncertainty, risk is inherent across all economic activities. Helping to combat this, finance offers tools and instruments to manage, hedge, and mitigate the most threatening

and potentially devastating of these risks. Insurance, derivatives, and other financial products enable businesses and individuals to protect themselves from unforeseen events, allowing them to focus on their core activities with a greater sense of security.

- **Capital Formation:** Capital is the lifeblood of entrepreneurship and business expansion. Without adequate access to capital, promising ideas and startups would struggle to materialize. Finance facilitates capital formation by channeling savings from individuals and institutions towards investment opportunities, fueling economic development and encouraging innovation.
- **Liquidity and Flexibility**: Financial markets and institutions provide liquidity, ensuring that assets can be converted into cash upon demand. This liquidity promotes investor confidence and fosters a dynamic economic environment, where participants can adjust their positions and respond swiftly to changing market conditions.
- **Economic Growth and Employment:** Sound financial systems stimulate economic growth by mobilizing savings and efficiently deploying them into productive investments. As economies grow, businesses expand. As a result, there emerges an increased demand for labor and a rise in employment opportunities.
- **Intermediation:** Finance plays an intermediary role, connecting those with surplus capital (savers) to those in need of funds (borrowers). Banks, financial institutions, and capital markets act as intermediaries, enabling efficient capital flow and promoting a balanced distribution of resources.
- **Facilitating Trade and Commerce:** Global trade heavily relies on finance, especially in cross-border transactions. Letters of credit, trade finance, and currency exchange services play a critical role in bolstering global trade and commerce, nurturing economic integration and collaborative efforts among nations.
- **Government Funding and Fiscal Policy:** Governments rely on finance to fund public projects from which we all benefit, most notably infrastructure development, education, and healthcare.

Efficient tax collection and fiscal policy help maintain a stable economy and provide essential services to citizens.

- **Wealth Management and Retirement Planning:** Finance plays a central role in effectively managing and expanding individual wealth. Various investment vehicles, such as stocks, bonds, and mutual funds, help individuals plan for their retirement and achieve long-term financial goals.
- **Economic Stability and Monetary Policy**: Central banks and monetary authorities utilize finance as a tool to regulate money supply, control inflation, and stabilize the economy. By influencing interest rates and implementing monetary policy, banks aim to promote sustainable economic growth and prevent extreme fluctuations.
- **Technological Advancements:** Finance has embraced technological innovations, leading to the emergence of fintech and digital banking solutions. These advancements have expanded financial access, improved payment systems, and democratized financial services, benefitting individuals and businesses globally.

WHAT WENT WRONG WITH THE FINANCIAL SYSTEM?

Since the commencement of industrialization, the financial system has been the backbone of modern economies, facilitating the allocation of capital, enabling investment, and supporting economic growth. However, it is not without its flaws and vulnerabilities, which became glaringly evident during the 2008 global financial crisis and subsequent financial disturbances. Several key factors contributed to what went wrong with the financial system, and looking at some of them can help equip us with a more nuanced and informed perspective of the financial system.

- **Subprime Mortgage Crisis:** One of the major triggers of the 2008 financial crisis was the rapid expansion of subprime mortgages. These were loans given to borrowers with poor credit histories, often with adjustable interest rates. As the housing market boomed, these risky mortgages were bundled together and sold as complex financial products known as mortgage-backed securities (MBS) and collateralized debt obligations (CDOs). When housing prices declined and subprime borrowers defaulted end masse, these securities lost value, leading to significant losses for financial institutions holding them.

- **Excessive Risk-Taking:** The financial system experienced a culture of excessive risk-taking and short-term profit maximization. Financial institutions, driven by the pursuit of higher profits, took on more and more risk without adequately assessing potential downsides. The use of complex financial instruments and derivatives further magnified risk and made it difficult for regulators to fully understand and mitigate potential threats.
- **Lack of Regulation and Oversight:** The financial industry witnessed deregulation and inadequate oversight in the years leading up to the crisis. Financial institutions engaged in practices that circumvented existing regulations, allowing them to take on greater risk without adequate capital reserves. Additionally, the regulatory framework failed to keep up with the evolution of complex financial products and did not effectively monitor systemic risks.
- **Too Big to Fail:** Some financial institutions became so large and interconnected that their potential failure was deemed a systemic risk to the entire financial system. This perception led to a moral hazard where these institutions knew they would likely be bailed out by governments if they faced imminent collapse. Consequently, it encouraged even riskier behavior, as the potential consequences of failure were mitigated by the expectation of government support.
- **Shadow Banking:** The rise of the shadow banking system, which includes non-bank financial intermediaries engaging in activities like traditional banks, added to the instability. These institutions operated with less stringent regulations, allowing them to take on substantial risks with limited oversight. When problems arose in this less transparent sector, it had significant spillover effects on the broader financial system.
- **Inadequate Risk Management:** Many financial institutions lacked or otherwise neglected the appropriate risk management practices and

failed to accurately assess the potential consequences of their actions. Risk models proved inadequate in forecasting extreme events, and there was a general underestimation of correlation risk between different assets and markets.

- **Herding Behavior:** In the lead-up to the crisis, there was a herd mentality among investors and financial institutions, with many following the same investment strategies and seeking similar assets. This amplified market volatility and increased systemic risks as large segments of the financial system were exposed to similar vulnerabilities.
- **Lack of Transparency:** The complexity of financial products, such as MBS and CDOs, made it difficult for investors and regulators to fully understand the risks associated with these instruments. Lack of transparency led to erroneously priced assets and increased uncertainty, contributing to market panic during the crisis.
- **Global Interconnectedness:** The financial system's increasing global interconnectedness meant that problems in one part of the world could quickly spread to other regions. The interconnectedness amplified the impact of the crisis and made coordination among international regulators challenging.
- **Behavioral Biases:** Human behavioral biases, such as overconfidence and herding, played a significant role in driving the irrational exuberance and excessive risk-taking leading up to the crisis. These biases led investors and financial institutions to overlook warning signs and engage in unsustainable practices.

Overall, what went wrong with the financial system can be attributed to a combination of factors, including the subprime mortgage crisis, excessive risk-taking, inadequate regulation and oversight, "too big to fail" mentality, shadow banking vulnerabilities, poor risk management practices, herding behavior, lack of transparency, global interconnectedness, and behavioral biases. Addressing these issues requires a comprehensive and coordinated effort from governments, regulators, financial institutions, and policymakers to build a more resilient and stable financial system.

HOW THE WORLD OF FINANCE CAN REFLECT SOCIETAL VALUES

As a pillar of modern societies, finance has exerted a profound impact on various aspects of human life, shaping economies, businesses, and individual well-being. It holds the potential to not only drive economic growth and prosperity but also to reflect and reinforce societal values. Historically, however, the financial sector has faced criticisms for its detachment from societal concerns, instead maintaining an overwhelming focus on maximizing profits and shareholder value. In the past few years, an increasing acknowledgment has emerged regarding the necessity for finance to assume a more substantial role in promoting sustainable development, social equity, and ethical conduct in business. In this way, finance can maintain pace with current trends in society. Such approaches to this new demand may include:

- **Ethical investing:** One way the finance industry can align with societal values is through ethical investing. This approach involves directing capital towards companies and projects that adhere to environmental, social, and governance (ESG) principles. By considering not only financial returns but also the impact on the environment and society more holistically, ethical investing empowers investors to make decisions that align with their values. Even more importantly, companies that prioritize sustainability, social responsibility, and ethical practices are increasingly sought after by conscientious investors, thereby driving positive change in the corporate world.
- **Socially responsible lending and financing:** Financial institutions have the power to influence the allocation of resources by providing loans and financing to various entities. Aligning their lending practices with societal values means supporting ventures that have a positive impact on communities and avoiding funding projects that harm the environment or exploit vulnerable populations. Banks, credit unions, and other lenders can integrate social and environmental risk

assessments into their decision-making processes to promote sustainable and equitable development.

- **Promotion of diversity and inclusion**: Societal values emphasize the importance of diversity, equity, and inclusion. The financial sector can take steps to ensure equal opportunities for all individuals, regardless of their background or identity. This includes promoting diversity within their own workforce, breaking down barriers hindering marginalized communities from accessing financial services, and supporting businesses owned by underrepresented or minority groups. By fostering an inclusive environment, financial institutions can play a crucial role in reducing societal inequalities.
- **Support for social entrepreneurship:** Social entrepreneurs are individuals or organizations that seek to create positive social and environmental impacts while maintaining financial viability. Supporting these ventures through funding and mentorship can catalyze innovative solutions to pressing societal challenges. By encouraging social entrepreneurship, the finance industry contributes to sustainable development and the betterment of society.
- **Transparency and accountability:** Financial institutions need to prioritize transparency and accountability in their operations. This includes clear and understandable communication with customers and stakeholders regarding financial products, risks, and fees. Transparent practices build trust and confidence in the financial sector and align with the paramount values of honesty and integrity.
- **Long-term thinking and sustainability:** In recent years, driven by the prevalence of influential individuals such as Greta Thunberg, social values increasingly have increasingly emphasized long-term thinking and sustainable practices over short-term gains. The finance industry can support this shift by rewarding companies that adopt sustainable business models and penalizing those that prioritize immediate profits at the expense of the environment and society. Encouraging long-term investment strategies also aligns with the broader societal objective of building resilient and stable economies.

- **Financial education and literacy:** Improving financial education and literacy among the general population is a crucial step in aligning the world of finance with the ever-changing societal values. When individuals understand how financial systems work, they can make informed decisions about their own finances and investments and help cultivate an empowered society that actively shapes the financial sector.
- **Advocacy and engagement:** Finance professionals and institutions can influence policy and advocate for regulatory changes that align with societal values. By actively engaging with policymakers and advocating for sustainable, equitable, and ethical financial practices, the finance industry can drive systemic change and create a positive impact on society.

In summary, the world of finance has a significant role to play in reflecting and promoting societal values. By embracing ethical investing, socially responsible lending, diversity and inclusion, support for social entrepreneurship, transparency, long-term thinking, financial education, and advocacy, the finance industry can become a powerful force for positive change. By integrating societal values into financial decision-making processes, we can build a more equitable, sustainable, and socially conscious world for future generations.

VENTURE CAPITAL

Venture capital is a form of private equity financing that provides funding to early-stage or emerging companies with high growth potential. These startups often face significant challenges in securing traditional bank loans due to their limited operating history and uncertain prospects. In such cases, venture capitalists (VCs) step in to fill the funding gap and support these companies in their early stages. VCs typically invest in exchange for an equity stake in the company, allowing them to share in the potential rewards when the startup becomes successful.

The role of venture capital goes beyond just providing financial capital. VCs often bring their expertise, industry knowledge, and valuable connections to the table. They actively engage with the startups they invest in, offering strategic guidance and mentoring to help them grow and achieve their business objectives. Moreover, venture capitalists are willing to take on higher risks in their investments, as they understand that not all startups will succeed. Their diversified investment portfolio allows them to absorb potential losses from unsuccessful ventures while benefiting significantly from the rare successes that yield substantial returns.

Investing in venture capital can be an attractive option for investors seeking high returns on their capital. However, you must understand that venture capital investments are illiquid and have longer time horizons compared to traditional investments. It may take several years for a startup to mature and reach a point of exit, such as through an initial public offering or acquisition, where the VC can realize their investment gains. Consequently, venture capital is often considered a long-term and patient investment strategy for those willing to accept the associated risks and potential delays in realizing profits.

The presence of venture capital plays a significant role in fostering innovation and driving economic growth. By funding early-stage companies with innovative ideas, VCs enable the development of groundbreaking technologies and products that can disrupt existing industries or create entirely new ones. This injection of capital and support can accelerate the growth of startups, allowing them to scale rapidly and compete with established players. Additionally, successful venture-backed companies can create jobs, stimulate economic activity, and contribute to the overall advancement of society. In this way, venture capital serves as a catalyst for fostering entrepreneurship and driving progress in the business world.

BUSINESS PLANS: WHAT ARE THEY, REALLY?

A business plan is a comprehensive and structured document that outlines the strategy and objectives of a new or existing business. It serves as a roadmap for entrepreneurs, providing a clear direction and framework for their venture. Developing a business plan should not be thought of as a chore; it is an essential part of any business and will take center stage whenever you pitch for external funding. The first key component of a business plan is the executive summary, which provides a concise overview of the company's mission, products or services, target market, and financial projections. Following the executive summary, the business plan delves into a detailed analysis of the business's market research, industry analysis, and competitive landscape. It outlines the organization's structure, management team, and marketing strategies, highlighting how the company will position itself in the market and attract customers. Additionally, the business plan includes a comprehensive financial section, detailing the projected revenue, expenses, and cash flow for the next few years, as well as potential risks and mitigation strategies. Overall, a well-crafted business plan is essential for attracting investors, guiding decision-making, and ensuring the long-term success of a business.

A successful business plan also incorporates a thorough operational plan that outlines the day-to-day functions and processes necessary for the company to achieve its goals. This section defines the production methods, distribution channels, and supplier relationships, providing a clear understanding of how the business will deliver its products or services to customers efficiently. Furthermore, a robust marketing and sales strategy is a crucial aspect of the plan, detailing the promotional activities, pricing strategies, and sales tactics to reach the target audience effectively. The financial projections included in the business plan are not only useful for attracting potential investors but also for the internal management of the company. They enable entrepreneurs to set measurable goals, track progress, and make data-driven decisions. A well-thought-out business plan is not only a document to be presented to external stakeholders but also a dynamic tool that business owners can continuously refine and adapt as their venture grows and evolves.

CHAPTER SIX

BUSINESS INSURANCE

Business insurance refers to a set of insurance policies that are designed to protect businesses from financial losses and other risks associated with various unexpected events or circumstances. As mentioned earlier, embarking on a business venture *without* the support of insurance would be an immensely daunting prospect; we should be grateful that this comfort blanket exists! Indeed, the advantages it provides are far ranging and will provide support in the event of many occurrences that you will likely fear. It provides coverage for property damage, liability, employee-related risks, and other potential threats that could impact a company's operations and financial stability. Business insurance aims to provide peace of mind to business owners by transferring the financial burden of certain losses to an insurance provider.

THE PURPOSE OF BUSINESS INSURANCE

Business insurance serves as a tool for safeguarding a company's assets, finances, and reputation against potential risks and liabilities. It serves several essential functions, including (but not limited to):

- **Risk Mitigation:** Business insurance helps to mitigate the financial impact of unexpected events, such as natural disasters, fires, theft, or accidents. Such events are devastating enough without having to worry about their impact on our hard-earned business. By having insurance coverage, businesses can recover more quickly and continue their operations even in the face of adversity.
- **Legal Compliance:** Many forms of business insurance, such as workers' compensation and professional liability insurance, are legally required in most jurisdictions. Maintaining adequate coverage ensures that a business operates within the bounds of the law. Of

course, this may be an area in which you wish to seek out more personalized information regarding your area of operation.

- **Protection of Assets:** Business insurance provides coverage for physical assets, such as buildings, equipment, inventory, and furniture. In the case of damage or loss, your insurance policy will help your business replace or—if possible—repair these assets without incurring significant financial burdens.
- **Liability Coverage:** Business insurance encompasses liability coverage, safeguarding the company against claims and legal actions arising from alleged negligence, bodily injury, property damage, and similar incidents. This prevents potential financial ruin resulting from costly legal battles and settlements.
- **Employee Protection:** Insurance policies like workers' compensation and employee health insurance benefit both the business *and* its employees. They provide financial support and medical coverage to employees injured on the job, enhancing the company's reputation as a responsible employer.
- **Business Continuity:** In the event of a significant loss or interruption to operations, such as a fire or natural disaster, business interruption insurance can provide funds to cover ongoing expenses and help the business stay afloat until it can resume normal operations.
- **Contractual Obligations:** Some businesses may require specific insurance coverage to fulfill contractual obligations with clients, vendors, or landlords. Having the necessary insurance policies in place ensures the business can enter into agreements with confidence. This naturally varies on a case-by-case basis, so it is worth conducting some research or seeking the help of a qualified professional to see whether this concern applies to you.
- **Peace of Mind:** It may sound superfluous, but you cannot underestimate the importance of peace of mind when it comes to entrepreneurship. Business owners invest time, effort, and capital in building and growing their ventures. Business insurance provides peace of mind, knowing that the company is protected against unforeseen risks and challenges.

In summary, business insurance plays a vital role in safeguarding a company's assets, financial stability, and reputation. By providing coverage for various risks and liabilities, it allows business owners to focus on their core activities with confidence, knowing that they have a safety net in place should the unexpected occur.

TYPES OF BUSINESS INSURANCE

Business insurance is a vital tool that helps protect companies from financial losses and potential liabilities that may arise during their operations. There are various types of business insurance, each designed to address different risks and needs. Some of the common types of business insurance—which you may need to understand ahead of embarking on your entrepreneurial journey—include:

- **General Liability Insurance:** This type of insurance provides coverage for third-party claims of bodily injury, property damage, and personal injury that occur on your business premises or as a result of your business operations.
- **Property Insurance:** Property insurance protects your business's physical assets, such as buildings, equipment, inventory, and furniture, against damage or loss due to events like fire, theft, vandalism, or natural disasters.
- **Business Interruption Insurance:** Also known as business income insurance, business interruption insurance helps replace lost income and covers ongoing expenses if your business operations are temporarily disrupted due to a covered event, like a fire or natural disaster.
- **Professional Liability Insurance:** Commonly referred to as errors and omissions (or E&O) insurance, this coverage protects businesses and professionals from claims of negligence, errors, or omissions that result in financial losses for clients or customers.
- **Cyber Liability Insurance**: With the increasing reliance on technology in modern society, this insurance helps businesses in the

event of data breaches, cyberattacks, or other cyber incidents that may lead to financial losses or reputation damage.

- **Workers' Compensation Insurance:** This type of insurance—which is required by law in many jurisdictions—provides coverage for medical expenses and lost wages for employees who suffer work-related injuries or illnesses.
- **Commercial Auto Insurance:** If your business uses vehicles for operations, commercial auto insurance provides coverage for physical damage and liability in case of accidents involving your company vehicles.
- **Product Liability Insurance:** Manufacturers, distributors, and retailers can benefit from product liability insurance, which offers coverage for claims related to injuries or damages caused by a faulty product your business produced or sold.
- **Employment Practices Liability Insurance (EPLI):** This insurance protects businesses from claims related to employment practices issues, such as wrongful termination, discrimination, sexual harassment, or other workplace-related claims.
- **Director and Officer (D&O) Insurance**: D&O insurance provides coverage for company directors and officers against legal actions brought against them for alleged wrongful acts while performing their corporate duties.
- **Key Person Insurance:** This insurance covers key employees or individuals whose loss could have a significant financial impact on the company. It helps the business manage the financial repercussions of losing a crucial team member.
- **Fidelity Bonds:** Also known as employee dishonesty coverage, fidelity bonds serve to protect a business against losses resulting from fraudulent activities by employees.

The specific insurance needs of a business may vary depending on factors such as its size, industry, location, and the nature of its operations. It is essential that you, as a business owner, work proactively with insurance professionals or agents to ensure that your insurance coverage best suits *your* unique requirements and risk exposure.

ASSESSING BUSINESS INSURANCE NEEDS

Having the right insurance coverage is vital for every business, ensuring safeguarding against unforeseen risks and potential financial hardships. Determining your business's insurance requirements entails a meticulous analysis of industry-related hazards, company scale, workforce size, and operational characteristics. Here is a flexible four-step plan that I have designed to help you assess your business insurance needs effectively.

1. **Identify Potential Risks:** Begin by conducting a comprehensive risk assessment of your business. Consider the various types of risks your company may face, such as property damage, liability claims, employee injuries, business interruption, and cyber threats. Analyze the specific risks that are prevalent in your industry and region. By understanding these risks, you can better prioritize and address the most critical insurance needs.
2. **Evaluate Legal Requirements:** Next, familiarize yourself with the insurance requirements mandated by law for businesses in your jurisdiction. Certain types of insurance, such as workers' compensation or professional liability coverage, may be legally required depending on your location and industry. Compliance with these regulations is essential to avoid potential fines and legal complications.
3. **Review Existing Coverage:** If your business already has insurance coverage, conduct a thorough review of your existing policies. Ensure that your current coverage aligns with your business's evolving needs. As your company evolves, your insurance requirements may also shift. Additionally, you should check for any overlaps or gaps in coverage that may leave your business exposed to risks.
4. **Consult with an Insurance Professional:** Assessing business insurance needs can be complex, especially if you are not familiar with insurance policies and industry standards. Consider consulting with an experienced insurance professional or broker who can provide

personalized guidance. They can help you navigate through various insurance options, tailor coverage to your specific business needs, and secure competitive quotes.

In summary, taking the time to assess your business insurance needs is crucial for safeguarding your company's financial well-being. By identifying potential risks, complying with legal requirements, reviewing existing coverage, and seeking professional advice, you can ensure that your business is adequately protected against unforeseen events and liabilities. Remember that business insurance is an investment in the long-term stability and success of your enterprise; this is *not* a step to skip, unless you want to risk regretting this further down the line.

CHOOSING THE RIGHT INSURANCE PROVIDER

Selecting the best-suited insurance provider is a monumental choice that severely impacts your financial security and sense of general wellbeing. Amidst the multitude of insurance companies competing for your business, it is essential to conduct thorough research to identify the best fit for your requirements. You may wish to adopt the step-by-step approach I have outlined below.

1. Begin by assessing the company's reputation and financial robustness. Seek out insurers with a proven history of satisfying customers and a consistent record of meeting financial obligations promptly. Consult ratings from impartial rating agencies, as these evaluations provide insights into the company's stability and ability to fulfill claims. An insurance provider with sound financial footing is more likely to manage your claims efficiently and maintain stability during challenging periods.

2. Next, examine the coverage options available from the insurance provider. Different insurers offer varying levels of coverage, policy features, and additional options. Ensure that the insurance policies align with your specific needs, whether you require health, auto,

home insurance, or other types of coverage. Scrutinize the available choices and select the one providing comprehensive protection at a reasonable cost.

3. Evaluate the insurer's customer service and claims handling procedures. Exceptional customer service can prove invaluable when you need to initiate a claim or seek clarifications about your policy. Gauge the company's responsiveness and willingness to assist customers by reviewing feedback from current or past policyholders. A proactive and supportive insurance provider can streamline the claims process and provide solace during challenging situations.

4. Lastly, compare insurance quotes from multiple providers to uncover competitive rates. While price shouldn't be the sole determinant, it remains a pivotal factor to consider. Request quotes for identical coverage levels from different insurers and analyze the costs and advantages offered by each. Keep in mind that the least expensive option may not always be the most suitable, as inadequate coverage or subpar service could lead to higher costs over time.

Overall, choosing the right insurance provider requires careful consideration of factors such as reputation, coverage options, customer service, and pricing. By conducting thorough research and weighing the pros and cons of different insurers, you can make an informed decision that ensures you receive the protection you need and deserve. Remember, insurance is a long-term commitment, so investing time in finding the right provider now can save you from potential headaches and financial hardships in the future.

CHALLENGES AND TRENDS IN BUSINESS INSURANCE

Business insurance is a crucial aspect of risk management for all companies, regardless of industry. It serves as a shield against unforeseen circumstances and financial liabilities that may unavoidably arise due to accidents, lawsuits, property damage, natural disasters, and other potential risks. However, the landscape of business insurance is continuously evolving, presenting numerous challenges and trends that both insurers and businesses must address to ensure adequate coverage and incorporate sustainable risk management strategies.

CHALLENGES IN BUSINESS INSURANCE:

- **Emerging Risks:** As businesses evolve and adopt new technologies and practices, new risks emerge. Cybersecurity threats, intellectual property infringement, environmental risks, and a damaged reputation through social media are all examples of emerging risks that traditional insurance policies may not adequately cover.
- **Globalization:** As businesses continue to expand their operations to a more global client base, insurance must become more complex. Ensuring compliance with different regulatory environments, understanding local insurance requirements, and managing risks across borders pose challenges for insurers and businesses alike. Again, this is something that varies on a case-by-case basis, and you should set aside time to conduct the pertinent research ahead of any overseas expansion.
- **Coverage Costs:** Rising insurance premiums and deductibles can strain a company's budget, especially for small and medium-sized enterprises. Balancing coverage needs with affordability becomes a significant challenge for businesses.
- **Underinsurance and Over insurance:** Finding the right balance between adequate coverage and overextending insurance protection is crucial. Underinsurance can leave a business vulnerable to significant financial losses, while over insurance can lead to unnecessary expenses.
- **Claims Management:** Timely and fair claims processing is critical for businesses to recover from losses efficiently. However, disputes

over coverage, delays in processing, and disputes with insurers can create additional stress for businesses during challenging times.

- **Lack of Understanding:** Business owners may not fully grasp the complexity of insurance policies, leading to misunderstandings about what is covered and what isn't. This lack of understanding can result in unpleasant surprises when a claim needs to be filed.
- **Evolving Legal and Regulatory Landscape**: Changes in laws and regulations can impact insurance requirements and coverage options. Staying updated with these changes can be challenging for businesses and insurers.

TRENDS IN BUSINESS INSURANCE

- **Customization and Flexibility:** To meet the diverse needs of businesses, insurers are moving towards more customizable insurance products. Modular policies that allow businesses to tailor coverage to their specific risks are becoming increasingly popular.
- **Data and Analytics:** Insurers are leveraging advanced data analytics to assess risks more accurately and determine appropriate premium rates. This data-driven approach also helps in identifying emerging risks and designing innovative insurance solutions.
- **Cyber Insurance:** With the increasing frequency and severity of cyber-attacks, cyber insurance has gained prominence. It covers losses arising from data breaches, cyber extortion, and other cyber incidents.
- **Parametric Insurance:** This type of insurance pays out a predetermined amount when specific trigger events occur, such as natural disasters or catastrophic events. It provides quicker payouts and reduces the administrative burden of traditional claims processing.
- **Climate Risk Insurance:** As climate change impacts become more evident, businesses are seeking insurance solutions to mitigate the financial consequences of extreme weather events and climate-related damages.

- **Peer-to-Peer Insurance:** This emerging trend involves groups of businesses coming together to self-insure each other for specific risks, bypassing traditional insurers and reducing costs.
- **Usage-Based Insurance (UBI):** UBI utilizes telematics and other technology to monitor business activities and charge premiums based on actual usage, offering potential cost savings for companies with safe operating practices.
- **Environmental, Social, and Governance (ESG) Factors**: Insurers are increasingly considering ESG criteria when underwriting policies. Businesses with strong ESG practices may receive favorable rates and terms, promoting sustainable business practices.

In conclusion, the landscape of business insurance is constantly evolving, and with it comes both challenges and exciting trends. Businesses need to stay informed about the changing risk landscape and work closely with insurers to design comprehensive and tailored insurance strategies that protect their assets, employees, and stakeholders effectively. Embracing technological advancements and innovative insurance solutions can provide businesses with a competitive edge in an increasingly complex and uncertain world.

CHAPTER SEVEN

MONEY AND CURRENCY

THE HISTORICAL ORIGINS AND EVOLUTION OF MONEY AND CURRENCY

As a concept, money can be traced back to the ancient barter system through which people exchanged goods and services directly. While broadly successful, this system suffered from somewhat inevitable limitations. Most notably, it required a double coincidence of wants. In other words, both parties (the giver and the receiver) both had to want what the other had to offer them. This, of course, limits the reach of any system. To overcome these challenges, civilizations began to adapt commodities with intrinsic value as mediums of exchange. Almost 5,000 years ago in ancient Mesopotamia, for example, clay tablets served as an early form of money, representing agricultural goods and resources. Similarly, the Ancient Egyptians normalized grain as a medium of exchange, while the Chinese Shang Dynasty (circa 1600-1046 BCE) used cowrie shells. These early forms of money laid the foundation for the evolution of currency.

The emergence of metal coins around the 6th century BCE marked a significant milestone in the evolution of what we now recognize as money. In what is present-day Turkey, the Lydians are credited with introducing the first standardized metal coins. These early coins were made from electrum, an alloy of gold and silver. The use of metal coins spread rapidly throughout ancient Greece, Rome, and other parts of the world, offering greater convenience and consistency in trade. As remains true to this day, coins bore the insignia of the issuing authority, adding an element of trust and legitimacy to the currency.

As civilizations expanded and trade routes connected distant regions, the need for a more practical and portable medium of exchange became evident. This led to the development of paper money during the Tang Dynasty in 7th-century China. Merchants and travelers deposited their valuable goods with local authorities and received paper certificates as proof of their holdings. These certificates could then be exchanged for goods and services within the region. The concept of paper money gradually spread along trade routes, reaching the Middle East and Europe by the 13th century, significantly facilitating cross-border transactions and spurring economic growth.

The 17th century saw the establishment of the world's first central banks, such as the Bank of England (1694). These institutions issued standardized banknotes, backed by reserves of precious metals like gold and silver. However, as economies expanded and trade flourished, the gold standard proved increasingly impractical, leading to the eventual abandonment of gold-backed currencies in the 20th century. With the advent of electronic banking and digital transactions, money has become even more abstract, existing mainly as electronic records in computer systems. The continuous evolution of money reflects the ever-changing needs of human society and its ongoing quest for a more efficient and reliable means of exchange.

DEFINITION OF MONEY

Money is a fundamental concept in modern economy, serving as a medium of exchange, unit of account, store of value, and standard of deferred payment. It represents a widely accepted and standardized form of payment that facilitates transactions and simplifies economic activities. In its essence, money is a tool that allows individuals and societies to overcome the limitations of barter systems by providing a more efficient means of conducting trade and measuring the value of goods and services.

First and foremost, money serves as a medium of exchange, meaning it acts as an intermediary in transactions. Rather than engaging in direct barter, where goods are exchanged for other goods, individuals can use money to buy and sell goods and services with ease. This greatly simplifies trade by eliminating the need for a double coincidence of wants, where both parties in a transaction must desire what the other has to offer.

Secondly, money functions as a unit of account. It provides a standardized way to measure and compare the value of various goods and services. By assigning prices to items in monetary terms, individuals can easily assess the worth of different products and make informed decisions about their purchases and investments. This common unit of measurement fosters transparency, efficiency, and stability in economic interactions.

Additionally, money serves as a store of value. This means that it can be saved and held over time to be used for future purchases or investment opportunities. Unlike perishable or rapidly depreciating goods, money's durability and relative stability make it a reliable tool for preserving purchasing power. Individuals can accumulate wealth by saving money for future needs or by investing it in assets that are expected to appreciate over time.

Lastly, money acts as a standard of deferred payment, enabling the settlement of debts and obligations over time. When individuals borrow money or engage in credit transactions, they are essentially promising to repay the debt in the future. Money allows these obligations to be settled in a predictable and consistent manner, facilitating the functioning of credit markets and financial systems.

Overall, money is an indispensable pillar of modern economies, serving as a medium of exchange, unit of account, store of value, and standard of deferred payment. Its widespread acceptance and adoption enable efficient trade, facilitate economic decision-making, and support the growth and development of societies. As financial systems evolve and technology advances, the concept of money continues to play a central role in shaping the dynamics of global commerce and finance.

THE IMPORTANCE OF MONEY IN MODERN SOCIETY

In modern society, the importance of money cannot be overstated. Money is the lifeblood that fuels our economy, drives progress, and influences almost all aspects of our daily lives. It serves as a medium of exchange, a store of value, and a measure of wealth. The significance of money can be seen from macroeconomic perspectives to individual micro-level decisions, impacting both nations and individuals alike. Below are the multifaceted reasons why money holds such a pivotal role in contemporary society.

- **Economic Stability:** Money provides the necessary stability for an economy to function efficiently. It enables governments to implement monetary policies, control inflation, and regulate interest rates. A stable economy leads to increased investments, job opportunities, and overall prosperity.
- **Standard of Living:** The availability of money directly influences our standard of living. With sufficient funds, individuals can access better healthcare, education, housing, and other essential services. Money empowers people to meet their basic needs and improve their quality of life.
- **Entrepreneurship and Innovation:** Money acts as a catalyst for entrepreneurship and innovation. Startups and businesses require capital to develop new products, technologies, and services that drive progress and societal advancements.
- **Social Mobility**: Money can be a tool for social mobility, allowing individuals from various backgrounds to improve their circumstances and achieve upward mobility. It provides opportunities for education and personal development, breaking the cycle of poverty for many.
- **Human Motivation:** Money serves as a significant motivator in the workforce. People work to earn money, supporting themselves and their families. Incentives like bonuses and salary increases inspire employees to strive for excellence and contribute more to their organizations.

- **Investment and Wealth Creation**: Money facilitates investment, leading to the creation of wealth. Through investments in stocks, real estate, and other financial instruments, individuals can accumulate wealth over time, providing financial security and retirement options.
- **Consumerism and Economic Growth:** Consumer spending drives economic growth. When people have money to spend, they create demand for goods and services, stimulating production and employment opportunities.
- **International Trade:** Money plays a crucial role in international trade, as it serves as the medium of exchange for global transactions. Currency exchange rates directly impact trade balances and influence a nation's economic competitiveness.
- **Philanthropy and Social Causes:** Money enables philanthropic endeavors and charitable donations. Wealthy individuals and organizations can support social causes, fund research, and address societal challenges, contributing to the greater good.
- **Government and Public Services:** Governments rely on money in the form of taxes to fund public services and infrastructure projects, such as education, healthcare, transportation, and defense. A well-funded government can better serve its citizens.
- **Economic Decision Making:** In the business world, money is central to decision-making processes. From budget allocation to pricing strategies, financial considerations underpin strategic choices that impact the success of companies and industries.
- **Global Influence:** Countries with strong economies and ample financial resources often wield significant influence on the international stage. Economic power translates into political leverage and can shape diplomatic relations and global policies.

In summary, money plays a pivotal role in modern society, touching nearly every aspect of our lives. Its importance spans from economic stability and individual prosperity to international relations and global influence. While money is undoubtedly essential, it is crucial to strike a balance, acknowledging its significance while also recognizing the importance of other values such as empathy, compassion, and social cohesion for a truly thriving and equitable society.

FUNCTIONS OF MONEY

Money serves several important functions in modern economies, facilitating the smooth operation of financial transactions and promoting economic growth. The most fundamental function of money is as a medium of exchange. In other words, money acts as a widely accepted intermediary in trade, allowing individuals and businesses to buy and sell goods and services without the need for bartering, which can be cumbersome and inefficient. By providing a universally accepted means of payment, money greatly enhances the efficiency of transactions and fosters economic specialization.

Another critical function of money is that it serves as a common measure of value for goods, services, and assets. With money as a unit of account, prices can be expressed in a standardized manner, making it easier for individuals and businesses to compare and evaluate the relative worth of different items. This function enables economic actors to make informed decisions about their financial activities, investments, and consumption patterns. While money has taken different forms throughout history, the advent of digital technologies and the rise of cryptocurrencies have introduced new possibilities for mediums of exchange. Cryptocurrencies, like Bitcoin and Ethereum, have gained traction as decentralized digital currencies, offering secure, borderless transactions with reduced reliance on traditional financial intermediaries. Despite the advancements, the concept of a medium of exchange remains a critical aspect of any functioning economy, facilitating trade, enabling growth, and shaping the dynamics of modern commerce.

Money also functions to retain wealth and sustain purchasing power for both individuals and businesses over an extended duration. Compared to perishable or deteriorating assets, money offers a reliable and relatively stable store of value. People can save money for future use or investment, and it serves as a hedge against uncertainty and unexpected expenses. Central banks play a crucial role in maintaining the stability of money as a store of value through monetary policies and measures to control inflation. In modern times, cryptocurrencies, most notably Bitcoin, have emerged as a new and unique type of store of value. Cryptocurrencies rely on blockchain technology and cryptographic principles to ensure scarcity and security. While their relatively short history makes their long-term stability uncertain, many investors view them as potential hedges against traditional fiat currencies and inflationary pressures. The growing interest in cryptocurrencies as stores of value reflects a shift in financial paradigms and the increasing digitization of wealth management.

Lastly, money functions as a standard of deferred payment. This means that money can be used to settle debts and obligations over time. Loans, mortgages, and other credit transactions rely on the understanding that money will retain its value in the future when the debt is repaid. This function encourages borrowing and lending activities, which can stimulate economic growth by financing investments and allowing individuals to smooth out their consumption patterns during times of financial strain.

Finally, the functions of money as a medium of exchange, unit of account, store of value, and standard of deferred payment are fundamental pillars of modern economies. These functions underpin economic activity, trade, investment, and financial stability, making money a vital component of our daily lives and the global economy. Over time, various units of account have been used throughout history, including commodities like gold, silver, and other precious metals. However, modern economies have largely shifted to fiat currencies issued by governments as their primary unit of account. Despite this, the rise of digital currencies and cryptocurrencies, like Bitcoin, has sparked debates about the future of money and the potential for alternative units of account in the digital age. Nonetheless, regardless of the specific currency or asset used, the concept of a unit of account remains integral to the functioning of economies worldwide, underpinning the entire financial system and facilitating economic interactions on a global scale.

TYPES OF MONEY

So far, we have learned that money is a medium of exchange that facilitates transactions and serves as a unit of account, a store of value, and a standard of deferred payment. Over the centuries, various forms of money have evolved to meet the needs of different societies and economies. Before you embark on your business journey, it will be worth having an overview of these types of money:

1. Commodity Money

Commodity money is currency that holds intrinsic value because it is made of a valuable commodity, such as gold, silver, or precious metals. Throughout history, and across countless a civilization, commodity money has been widely used as a medium of exchange and a store of value. Its tangible nature and scarcity make it appealing as a form of money that can withstand fluctuations in the economy and maintain its value over time.

Indeed, one of the primary advantages of commodity money is its resistance to inflation. Since the supply of the commodity is limited, the amount of money that can be created is constrained. This characteristic ensures that the value of commodity money remains relatively stable over time, providing a reliable unit of account for economic transactions. However, a downside to commodity money is the practicality of its handling and storage commodities. This partly explains its declining presence over time. As economies grew, carrying and securing large amounts of gold or silver became cumbersome and risky, leading to the development of representative money and eventually modern fiat currencies. Nonetheless, the concept of commodity money remains relevant in the context of precious metal investments and as a historical reference to the evolution of monetary systems. Understanding commodity money's role in shaping the foundations of today's financial systems offers us valuable insights into the nature of money and its enduring significance in economic exchanges.

2. Fiat Money

Fiat money is currency that has no intrinsic value and is not backed by a physical commodity like gold or silver. Instead, its value is derived from the trust and confidence of the people who use it as a medium of exchange and a store of value. In other words, fiat money has value because the government, through its legal tender laws and monetary policy, decrees it to be the official currency and people accept it as such for transactions. Fiat money is created and regulated by governments and central banks, which have the authority to issue and control the money supply. This control gives them the ability to manage economic conditions and implement monetary policies such as controlling inflation, stimulating economic growth, or stabilizing the currency exchange rate.

Key characteristics of fiat money:

- **No Intrinsic Value:** Unlike commodity money (such as gold or silver coins), fiat money has no inherent worth. Instead, its value is purely symbolic and exists wholly because people *believe* it to be valuable for trade.
- **Legal Tender:** Fiat money is recognized as the official currency within a country's borders and is accepted for all types of transactions by law. This also means that creditors must accept it as payment for debts.
- **Divisibility and Portability:** Fiat money is typically issued in various denominations, making it easily divisible into smaller units. This divisibility, along with its physical form (e.g., paper bills and coins with varying assigned values), makes it highly portable and convenient for everyday transactions.
- **Controlled Supply:** Governments and central banks have the authority to control the supply of fiat money. They can print more money or withdraw it from circulation based on economic needs and policy objectives.
- **Vulnerability to Inflation:** One of the drawbacks of fiat money is that its supply can be increased too rapidly, leading to inflation, which erodes its purchasing power over time. However, central banks try to

manage inflation and stabilize the value of the currency through various monetary policies.

The use of fiat money has become widespread globally since the 20th century, with most countries adopting this form of currency. Its acceptance relies on the trust and stability of the issuing government or central authority. If people continue to have faith in the stability of the government and its economic policies, fiat money remains a viable and practical medium of exchange. Nevertheless, the value and stability of fiat money are subject to economic, political, and social factors, which can influence its purchasing power and overall acceptance.

3. Representative Money

Representative money is a form of currency that represents a claim on a commodity or a reserve of value rather than being inherently valuable itself. In other words, representative money relies on a promise from a trusted entity, typically a government or a central bank, that it can be exchanged for a specific amount of a valuable commodity or resource. Historically, representative money emerged as a solution to the impracticality of carrying large quantities of heavy or valuable commodities for trade and transactions.

One of the most common forms of representative money is the gold standard, which prevailed in many economies during the 19th and early 20th centuries. Under the gold standard, paper currency was issued and backed by a fixed amount of gold held in reserve by the issuing authority. This system provided stability and confidence in the currency's value, as the paper money could always be redeemed for its equivalent in gold. However, as economies grew and faced the limitations of gold reserves, most countries eventually transitioned to fiat money.

Therefore, while representative money played a crucial role in the development of modern monetary systems, it has become less prevalent with the rise of fiat currencies. Nevertheless, the concept of representing value through a trustworthy entity remains significant, underpinning the stability and functionality of contemporary monetary systems worldwide. In today's financial landscape, the assurance of governments and central banks to manage their currencies responsibly and maintain their value is what reinforces the trust in paper money and digital currencies alike.

4. Digital Money

Digital money, also known as electronic money or e-money, refers to a form of currency that exists solely in electronic or digital form. It is a modern financial innovation that has transformed the way we conduct transactions, enabling swift, secure, and convenient payment methods in our increasingly digital world. Unlike physical cash or traditional banknotes, digital money exists only as digital data, stored and exchanged electronically.

Various forms of digital money exist, each holding its own underlying technology and use cases:

- **Digital Currencies:** These are cryptocurrencies like Bitcoin, Ethereum, and Ripple. Digital currencies are decentralized and use blockchain technology to facilitate secure and transparent transactions without the need for a central authority, such as a government or a bank.
- **Central Bank Digital Currencies (CBDCs):** Issued and regulated by central banks, CBDCs represent the digital form of a country's official currency. They retain the backing and stability of traditional fiat currencies while providing the benefits of digital transactions.
- **Electronic Funds Transfer (EFT):** EFT involves the electronic transfer of money between different financial institutions or individuals. Common examples include online bank transfers, wire transfers, and direct deposit payments.
- **Digital Wallets:** Also known as e-wallets or mobile wallets, digital wallets are applications or platforms that store various payment methods, such as credit cards, debit cards, and digital cash. They allow users to make purchases and payments using their smartphones or other devices. Google Pay and Apple Pay are well-known examples.

- **Prepaid Cards:** These are physical or virtual cards loaded with a specific amount of money, often used for online purchases or as an alternative to traditional debit or credit cards.

Advantages of Digital Money:

- ✓ **Convenience:** Digital money offers unparalleled convenience, allowing users to make instant transactions anytime, anywhere, without the need for physical cash or visiting a bank.
- ✓ **Security:** Encryption and authentication mechanisms ensure secure transactions, reducing the risk of counterfeiting and theft compared to physical cash.
- ✓ **Lower Transaction Costs:** Digital transactions generally incur lower fees compared to traditional payment methods, making it more cost-effective for both consumers and businesses.
- ✓ **Financial Inclusion**: Digital money can extend financial services to unbanked or underbanked populations, providing them with access to various financial services.
- ✓ **Global Accessibility:** With digital money, international transactions become more accessible and efficient, eliminating the need for currency conversions and reducing cross-border payment complexities.

Digital money continues to evolve, and its increasing adoption is likely to shape the future of finance and commerce. As technology advances and concerns are addressed, digital money is expected to become an integral part of the global financial landscape.

THE PSYCHOLOGY OF MONEY

Financial psychology presents a thought-provoking domain of study that delves into the cognitive, behavioral, and socio-cultural dimensions underlying individuals' cognition, utilization, and engagement with monetary resources. Within this scholarly arena, a leading area of study concerns the intriguing question of how our predispositions and actions concerning finances are molded by early developmental factors, personal encounters, and broader societal forces. At the core of the field is the notion that money—that is, money of any type outlined in the section above—is not just a medium of exchange; it carries emotional significance and represents security, success, and even self-worth for many people. This emotional attachment can lead to various financial decisions and behaviors that may not always align with rational economic choices.

Moreover, financial psychology delves into the concept of *money personalities*, which categorizes individuals based on their money-related behaviors and attitudes. Some people are natural savers, while others are impulsive spenders. Certain individuals even exhibit a tendency to experience feelings of anxiety or guilt around money matters. Understanding our own money personalities can be instrumental in improving our financial habits and overall wellbeing. It should come as no surprise, then, that financial advisors often take these factors into account when developing personalized strategies for their clients to achieve their financial goals.

Furthermore, the psychology of money highlights the impact of cognitive biases on financial decision-making. Decades of empirical psychological research has verified that human beings are susceptible to biases like loss aversion, where the fear of losing money outweighs the benefits of potential gains, leading to overly cautious behaviors. Similarly, confirmation bias can cloud judgment, causing individuals to seek information that supports their pre-existing beliefs about money, leading to potentially risky choices. Recognizing and addressing these biases can help people make more informed and objective financial decisions.

In summary, research and insights from the psychology of money shed light on the complex relationship between human behavior and financial matters. It underscores the need for financial education and awareness to navigate the challenges and pitfalls of managing money effectively. By understanding our monetary personalities, recognizing cognitive biases, and gaining insight into our emotional connections with money, we can foster healthier financial habits, make better investment choices, and ultimately work towards achieving greater financial security and wellbeing.

CHAPTER EIGHT

INNOVATION

Innovation is a crucial element in the success of any business. It is a driving force that allows organizations to adapt to changing environments and stay ahead of their competitors. However, it is regrettable that many small companies do not prioritize innovation, as evidenced by their reluctance to update a plethora of business features, ranging from their office furniture to their concepts of thinking.

Let's consider the former. It is not uncommon to walk into the premises of a business that has been in existence for over two decades and find that the owner has never bothered to renovate the place. This lack of investment in the physical environment of the business suggests a complacency and a resistance to change, which can almost immediately deter potential customers. Of course, the same can be true of an outdated website or social media presence, too (even more worryingly, these examples may cause customers to be unsure whether the business is still operating). All in all, such businesses are often stuck in outdated practices and fail to embrace new technology or design trends that could improve their overall performance and attract more customers.

While financial constraints are a possible reason for a lack of updating, some businesses may intentionally prefer to maintain the status quo. Such business owners believe that if a method has worked for them in the past, there is no need to change it, even if there are evident opportunities for improvement. This rigid mindset can severely limit the potential growth and development of the business, as it fails to capitalize on new ideas and approaches that could bring about positive change and, most importantly, new customers.

It is important for small companies to recognize the value of innovation and the impact it can have on their long-term success. Innovation goes beyond just updating physical aspects of the business; it\involves fostering a culture that encourages creativity and continuous improvement. By embracing new ideas and being open to change, small companies can position themselves better in a rapidly evolving business landscape and ensure their survival in the face of fierce competition.

DEFINING INNOVATION

Innovation refers to the process of introducing new ideas, methods, products, or services that bring about significant positive change and advancement. It is a driver of progress in various fields, spanning technology, business, science, and society. Innovations can emerge from groundbreaking research, creative thinking, or even simply combining already-existing concepts in novel, productive ways. They often result in increased efficiency, improved quality of life, and enhanced competitiveness in the global market. A successful innovation can constitute the foundations of a successful business of any size or nature.

At its core, innovation involves challenging the status quo and embracing a mindset that encourages experimentation and risk-taking. It requires individuals, teams, or organizations to be open to change and responsive to evolving demands. Successful innovators are not afraid to fail; they recognize that setbacks are an inherent part of the learning process and can lead to valuable insights. Moreover, innovation often involves collaboration among diverse groups, fostering an environment in which different perspectives can converge to develop groundbreaking solutions. In today's fast-paced and interconnected world, companies that prioritize innovation are more likely to adapt to changing market dynamics, stay ahead of competitors, and create lasting impacts. Moreover, innovation fosters inclusivity, as diverse perspectives and collaborations often lead to more comprehensive and impactful solutions. Governments and organizations must actively support and invest in research and development, education, and infrastructure to cultivate a culture of innovation that benefits society.

While innovation has brought about remarkable advancements, however, we ought to note that it also raises ethical and societal considerations. Responsible innovation requires a thoughtful approach that considers the potential consequences of new ideas or technologies. Striking a balance between progress and ethical considerations is crucial to ensure that innovations do not cause harm or perpetuate existing inequalities. By harnessing the power of innovation responsibly, humanity can unlock its potential for a brighter and more sustainable future.

THE IMPORTANCE OF INNOVATION IN VARIOUS FIELDS

It has been a fundamental aspect of human development and has played a crucial role in shaping societies, economies, and the overall advancement of civilization. In the modern world, innovation plays a crucial role in addressing complex challenges, such as climate change, healthcare issues, and resource scarcity. Technological innovations have revolutionized communication, transportation, and the way we conduct business. Furthermore, sustainable innovation has gained traction, emphasizing the importance of creating solutions that not only cater to current needs but also promote long-term ecological and social well-being. Embracing innovation allows societies to adapt, thrive, and stay ahead in an ever-changing and interconnected global landscape. Below, I outline some of the primary reasons which innovation is so central to the success of humanity.

- ✓ **Technological Advancements:** Innovation is at the core of technological advancements. It enables the development of new technologies, products, and services that can transform industries, improve living standards, and solve complex problems.
- ✓ **Economic Growth:** Innovation plays a significant role in stimulating economic growth. When businesses innovate, they create new markets and opportunities, leading to increased productivity, job creation, and higher competitiveness on a global scale.

- ✓ **Solving Global Challenges:** Many of the world's most pressing challenges, such as climate change, healthcare, poverty, and food security, require innovative solutions. Innovation encourages the development of sustainable practices and disruptive technologies to tackle these issues.
- ✓ **Enhancing Productivity and Efficiency:** In every sector, innovation can lead to streamlined processes and more efficient workflows. This results in reduced costs, increased output, and better utilization of resources.
- ✓ **Improving Quality of Life:** Innovations in healthcare, education, and technology can significantly enhance people's quality of life. Advancements in medical treatments, educational tools, and communication technologies have a direct positive impact on society.
- ✓ **Competitive Advantage:** In a competitive world, businesses that embrace innovation gain a competitive edge. By offering unique products or services, they can attract more customers and retain existing ones.
- ✓ **Adaptation to Change:** Innovating helps organizations adapt to changing market conditions, customer preferences, and technological advancements. It ensures that businesses remain relevant and resilient in dynamic environments.
- ✓ **Creativity and Exploration:** Innovation encourages creativity and exploration of new ideas. This fosters a culture of learning and continuous improvement, encouraging individuals and organizations to push boundaries and take calculated risks.
- ✓ **Inspiration for Future Generations:** Innovations inspire future generations to build upon existing knowledge and continue to advance society. Pioneering breakthroughs serve as a foundation for further progress in various fields.
- ✓ **Social Progress:** Innovations can drive positive social change and create more inclusive societies. For example, advancements in renewable energy, assistive technologies, and access to information can empower disadvantaged communities and bridge societal gaps.

- ✓ **Environmental Sustainability:** Innovative solutions are essential in addressing environmental challenges. Developing eco-friendly technologies and sustainable practices helps reduce the impact on the planet and preserve natural resources for future generations.
- ✓ **Research and Development**: Innovation drives research and development efforts in multiple disciplines, leading to discoveries that may have unforeseen applications in other areas, amplifying the overall progress of human knowledge.

Overall, innovation is a driving force behind progress and prosperity in various fields. It has the power to transform industries, solve global challenges, and improve the quality of life for people worldwide. Embracing a culture of innovation is crucial for organizations and societies to remain relevant and thrive in an ever-changing world.

INNOVATION IN BUSINESS AND ECONOMICS

Innovation in business and economics plays a crucial role in driving economic growth and shaping the future of industries. Businesses that embrace innovation are more likely to stay competitive and adapt to changing market demands. From technological advancements to process improvements, innovation fosters creativity and efficiency, allowing companies to develop groundbreaking products and services. Moreover, innovation is a catalyst for entrepreneurship, inspiring individuals to create their own ventures and contribute to economic development. Recall earlier in the book when we discussed the personal and technical qualities required to be a successful entrepreneur; creativity and innovation sit at the forefront of such skillsets.

It is important that we look beyond our own businesses, too. Indeed, innovation also has a profound impact on the overall economy. Pioneering ideas and disruptive technologies often lead to the establishment of new industries and the transformation of existing ones. This dynamic process generates job opportunities and stimulates consumer spending, driving economic expansion. Governments recognize the significance of innovation and often implement policies to incentivize research and development. In doing so, they establish an environment conducive to cultivating inventive endeavors and enticing capital infusion.

The digital revolution has been a driving force behind innovation in business and economics. The advent of the internet, artificial intelligence, big data, and blockchain technology has revolutionized the way companies operate and interact with their customers. E-commerce, for example, has transformed traditional retail, enabling businesses to reach global markets with greater ease and efficiency (as we discussed earlier when delving into the tremendous success of services like Amazon and Uber). Additionally, the integration of smart technologies and automation in manufacturing processes has improved productivity and product quality, consistency and manufacture speed.

To sustain innovation in business and economics, organizations must nurture a culture of continuous learning and informed risk-taking. Encouraging employees to think creatively and providing them with the resources, environment and support to experiment with new ideas is crucial. This is part of the reason that companies like Google and Innocent allow employees to work from beanbags, colorful pods, and lakeside benches; such environments are undeniably conducive to creative thinking and, therefore, innovation. Moreover, collaboration with academia and research institutions plays a notable role in fostering innovation, allowing businesses to tap into a pool of expertise in a flexible way, thus empowering them to stay at the forefront of cutting-edge developments. Overall, innovation remains the driving force behind economic progress, enabling businesses to thrive in an ever-evolving world.

INNOVATION IN TECHNOLOGY AND SCIENCE

Technological and scientific innovation has long been the driving force behind human progress, simultaneously shaping our current world and propelling us into the future. From communication and transportation to healthcare and energy production, technological advancements and scientific breakthroughs have not only made our lives more convenient and efficient but have also solved complex challenges that were once considered insurmountable. It is interesting to look deeper into the impact of these breakthroughs in various fields and sectors.

1. **Communication**: The internet and mobile technology have connected the world like never before, enabling instant access to information and facilitating global collaborations. Social media platforms have revolutionized the way we interact and share ideas, fostering a global community and promoting cultural exchange. Additionally, advancements in artificial intelligence and natural language processing have transformed the way we communicate with machines, opening new possibilities for automation and personalized experiences.

2. **Transportation**: Electric and autonomous vehicles are changing the landscape of transportation, reducing carbon emissions and increasing safety on the roads. Furthermore, the concept of Hyperloop and other high-speed transportation systems are promising faster and more efficient travel between cities, potentially reshaping urban living and regional economies.

3. **Healthcare**: Innovation in technology and science has played a pivotal role in improving diagnosis, treatment, and patient care. Medical imaging technologies, such as MRI and CT scans, have provided unprecedented insights into the human body, enabling early detection of diseases and precise interventions. Robotics and telemedicine have extended medical reach to remote areas, improving access to healthcare services for millions of people. Furthermore, groundbreaking discoveries in genomics and personalized medicine hold the promise of tailoring treatments to an individual's unique genetic makeup.

4. **Energy**: Renewable energy sources, such as solar, wind, and hydroelectric power, have gained momentum, offering sustainable alternatives to traditional fossil fuels. Advancements in battery technology have facilitated energy storage, making renewable energy sources more reliable and accessible. Moreover, the integration of smart grids and energy-efficient technologies has enhanced energy management and conservation, paving the way for a more sustainable future.

5. **Space Exploration:** In the field of space exploration, technological innovation has pushed the boundaries of human exploration beyond our planet. From reusable rockets to Mars missions, private and government entities are working together to uncover the mysteries of the cosmos and potentially find new habitats for humanity. The knowledge gained from space exploration also has practical applications on Earth, benefiting various industries and our understanding of the universe.

NETFLIX: REVOLUTIONIZING ENTERTAINMENT

In just a few short years, Netflix has become synonymous with entertainment, revolutionizing how people consume TV shows, movies, and documentaries. Founded in 1997 by Reed Hastings and Marc Randolph, Netflix started as a DVD rental-by-mail service, but it has since evolved into a global streaming giant. Its meteoric rise to prominence can be attributed to several key factors that have propelled it to the forefront of the entertainment industry.

1. The Streaming Revolution

In 2007, Netflix introduced its streaming service, forever changing the way people watch content. By providing instant access to a vast library of films and TV shows, Netflix tapped into the growing demand for on-demand entertainment. Gone were the days of waiting for DVDs to arrive in the mail; users could now stream their favorite shows and movies at any time, on any device with an internet connection. This convenience factor played a significant role in Netflix's rapid expansion.

2. Original Content Pioneers

Recognizing the need for differentiation in the highly competitive streaming market, Netflix became a trailblazer in producing original content. "House of Cards" marked its first major foray into original programming in 2013, followed by numerous other hugely popular and successful series such as "Stranger Things," "The Crown," and "Orange Is the New Black." By investing heavily in exclusive content, Netflix positioned itself as a destination for compelling, high-quality shows that couldn't be found elsewhere.

3. Personalization and Recommendation Algorithms

Netflix's ability to suggest content tailored to individual users' preferences has been a game-changer. By leveraging sophisticated recommendation algorithms, the platform delivers personalized content suggestions based on users' viewing history and preferences. This even includes changing the cover image for various shows based on the viewer's preferred genre! This not only keeps viewers engaged but also allows Netflix to promote a diverse range of content, increasing the chances of users discovering new shows and movies that they might enjoy.

4. Global Expansion

Netflix's success is not confined to the United States. The company has made significant efforts to expand its reach globally, making its service available in over 190 countries. By catering to international audiences with localized content and subtitles, Netflix has been able to break down geographical barriers and reach millions of subscribers worldwide.

5. Innovative Business Model

Netflix's subscription-based business model has proven to be highly successful. By offering different pricing tiers to suit varying needs and budgets, the platform attracts a broad audience. Moreover, the absence of ads during streaming sessions ensures an uninterrupted viewing experience, a welcome change for viewers who were tired of traditional cable television's ad-heavy approach.

6. Social and Cultural Impact

Beyond its business success, Netflix has had a profound social and cultural impact. It has popularized binge-watching, where viewers consume multiple episodes or an entire series in one sitting, leading to changes in storytelling and narrative structures. Additionally, Netflix has been at the forefront of promoting diversity and inclusivity in its content, representing a wide range of voices and perspectives.

THE FUTURE OF NETFLIX

As of my knowledge cutoff in September 2021, Netflix continues to face stiff competition from other streaming services like Amazon Prime Video, Disney+, HBO Max, and Hulu. In response, Netflix maintains its commitment to investing in original content, striking deals with top-tier creators, and diversifying its library to cater to an ever-expanding global audience.

While the streaming landscape continues to evolve, and new challenges may arise, there's no denying that Netflix has had a transformative impact on the way we consume entertainment. From pioneering streaming technology to reshaping how original content is produced and distributed, Netflix remains a powerhouse in the entertainment industry, and its influence is likely to be felt for years to come.

UBER: DISRUPTING THE TAXI INDUSTRY

Uber, the ride-hailing giant, has undeniably disrupted the taxi industry like never before. With its revolutionary platform, Uber has transformed the way people commute, challenging the traditional taxi model and reshaping the transportation landscape. Like Netflix, an innovative use of technology set Uber apart from the crowd of 'traditional' taxi operators. Through its user-friendly mobile app, passengers can request rides with just a few taps, eliminating the need for phone calls or hailing taxis on the street. This streamlined experience not only saves time but also enhances convenience, making it a preferred choice for millions of users worldwide.

Uber's pricing model has likewise been a game-changer. Instead of charging fixed rates like traditional taxis, Uber employs a dynamic pricing system based not only on distance, but also on demand and supply. This approach, known as surge pricing, enables Uber to cater to varying passenger needs while ensuring a more balanced distribution of drivers during peak times. Although controversial at times, this method allows Uber to remain competitive and responsive to real-time demand fluctuations, effectively meeting the transportation needs of urban dwellers and travelers alike.

Furthermore, Uber's emphasis on ensuring seamless driver-passenger interactions has been a driving force behind its success. Drivers are thoroughly vetted and rated by passengers after each trip, incentivizing them to provide excellent service. This rating system fosters accountability and encourages drivers to maintain high standards, ultimately enhancing the overall ride experience for passengers. Additionally, Uber's cashless payment system promotes security and convenience, as passengers do not need to carry physical currency, thereby reducing the risk of robbery or fraudulent transactions.

Finally, Uber's global expansion strategy has enabled it to reach previously underserved markets and revolutionize transportation options in cities around the world. The platform's scalability and adaptability have allowed Uber to localize its services, accommodating local regulations and cultural preferences while maintaining its core technological advantages. As a result, Uber has become a symbol of the sharing economy and a pioneer in the industry, challenging traditional taxi services and setting new standards for transportation accessibility and efficiency. With its commitment to innovation and customer-centric approach, Uber continues to disrupt the taxi industry and shape the future of urban mobility.

CHAPTER NINE

SUCCESSION PLANNING (BUY-SELL ARRANGEMENT)

WHAT IS BUY/SELL AGREEMENT?

A buy/sell agreement, also referred to as a buyout agreement or a business continuation agreement, is a legally binding contract that plays a vital role in managing and mitigating the potential turmoil and uncertainties that can arise from the sudden departure, disability, or death of a business owner or partner. This agreement serves as a strategic tool for businesses, particularly those with multiple owners or partners, to establish a clear framework for handling ownership transitions and ensuring the continuity and stability of the enterprise.

The core purpose of a buy/sell agreement is to provide a structured plan that outlines the terms and conditions for the potential buying and selling of ownership interests in the company or partnership. It comes into play when specific triggering events occur, such as the voluntary retirement of a partner, a partner's desire to sell their shares, the unexpected disability of a key stakeholder, or the unfortunate demise of an owner. By addressing these events in advance, a buy/sell agreement creates a roadmap for handling these critical situations in a manner that is agreeable to all parties, thereby reducing potential conflicts and uncertainties that may arise during emotionally charged and stressful circumstances.

Life insurance policies often play a significant role in funding buy/sell agreements. Business owners or partners can take out life insurance policies on each other, ensuring that in the event of a partner's death, the necessary funds are readily available to facilitate the buyout of the deceased partner's ownership interest. The insurance payout can be used to compensate the deceased partner's family or estate for their share of the business while allowing the surviving partners to retain full control and ownership of the company. This funding mechanism is especially crucial for businesses in which access to significant liquid cash might be limited, as it offers a reliable and immediate source of funds during a challenging time.

The buy/sell agreement also addresses the valuation method used to determine the price of the ownership interest being traded. Several valuation approaches can be employed, such as using the company's fair market value or book value, or following a predetermined formula agreed upon by all parties. Selecting the most appropriate valuation method is essential, given that it directly impacts the financial implications of the transaction and ensures fairness to all parties involved in the buy/sell arrangement.

Finally, the buy/sell agreement can include provisions related to disability buyouts. In the event of a partner's disabling injury or illness, the agreement can define the terms for buying out the disabled partner's shares, allowing for a smooth transition of ownership and management responsibilities to the remaining partners.

TYPES OF BUY/SELL AGREEMENTS

There are two main types of buy/sell agreements that many business owners opt for: the cross-purchase plan and the entity purchase plan (also known as the stock redemption plan).

1. Cross-Purchase Plan:

In a cross-purchase plan, each business owner takes out a life insurance policy on every other owner. If one of the owners passes away, the surviving owners receive the payout from the life insurance policy and use it to purchase the deceased owner's share of the business.

2. Entity Purchase (Stock Redemption) Plan:

The entity purchase plan involves each employee-owner entering into an agreement with the business to sell their interest in the company. As part of this agreement, the business purchases life insurance policies on each owner, paying the premiums and becoming the owner and beneficiary of the policies.

When an employee-owner passes away, their share of the business passes to their estate's heirs, and the business can use the death benefit from the insurance policy to buy the deceased owner's interest from the estate.

POTENTIAL BUSINESS BENEFITS OF A BUY/SELL AGREEMENT

- ✓ **Fair Market Value Exchange:** The agreement provides a clear method for determining the value of the business and facilitates a fair exchange when ownership changes hands.
- ✓ **Equitable and Orderly Transfer:** It ensures a smooth and fair transfer of wealth, ownership, and management within the company.
- ✓ **Tax Advantages:** Depending on the structure and specifics of the agreement, there may be potential tax benefits for the business and its owners.
- ✓ **Security for Heirs:** Heirs of the deceased owners are guaranteed a buyer for their inherited assets, which they might not have the expertise to manage effectively.
- ✓ **Financial Support for Estate Costs:** The agreement provides the heirs with the necessary cash to cover estate debts, expenses, and taxes, reducing financial burdens during an already challenging time.

POTENTIAL BENEFITS FOR BUSINESS PARTNERS AND EMPLOYEES

- ✓ **Ownership Stability:** The agreement ensures that the ownership remains in the hands of suitable individuals and prevents shares from passing to unsuitable or inexperienced parties.
- ✓ **Continuity for Stakeholders:** Customers, creditors, and employees can be confident in the company's continuity, knowing that the agreement will manage changes in ownership without disrupting operations.

IMPORTANCE OF BUY/SELL ARRANGEMENTS IN SUCCESSION PLANNING

Succession planning is a crucial aspect of any business or organization's long-term sustainability and continuity. It involves identifying and developing future leaders *within* the organization to ensure a seamless transition of responsibilities when key individuals leave or retire. One essential component of effective succession planning is the implementation of well-structured buy/sell arrangements. The importance of buy/sell arrangements in succession planning cannot be overstated, and here are some key reasons why they are critical:

- ✓ **Facilitating Smooth Transitions:** Buy/sell arrangements provide a clear roadmap for how the transfer of ownership and management will happen. By establishing predetermined terms and conditions, they minimize potential conflicts and uncertainties that could arise during the transition process.
- ✓ **Protecting Business Stability:** In the absence of a buy/sell agreement, the departure of a key stakeholder could lead to disruption and instability within the organization. Having a well-defined plan in place ensures that the business can continue to operate smoothly, even in challenging times.
- ✓ **Ensuring Fair Valuation:** Buy/sell agreements usually include provisions for valuing the business or the departing owner's share. This helps avoid disputes over the value of the company and ensures that all parties are treated fairly during the buyout process.
- ✓ **Retaining Key Employees:** An effectively structured buy/sell arrangement can provide incentives for key employees to stay with the organization in the knowledge that they could become future owners. This can increase employee loyalty and motivation.
- ✓ **Protecting Family Interests:** In family-owned businesses, a buy/sell agreement can be especially vital to prevent potential conflicts between family members who disagree over the distribution of assets and control of the business.

- ✓ **Funding the Transition:** Buy/sell arrangements can address the financial aspect of the succession plan by specifying how the departing owner's interest will be financed. This might involve insurance policies, installment payments, or external financing options.
- ✓ **Minimizing Tax Implications:** Properly structured buy/sell agreements can help minimize the tax burden for both the selling and purchasing parties, making the transition financially efficient.
- ✓ **Avoiding External Interference:** Without a buy/sell agreement, external parties, such as competitors or investors, may attempt to gain control of the business during a time of vulnerability, potentially harming the organization's interests.
- ✓ **Protecting Business Creditworthiness:** With a well-organized succession plan, lenders and stakeholders can have confidence in the company's long-term viability, which can positively impact creditworthiness and future growth opportunities.
- ✓ **Legal Compliance:** By formalizing the transfer of ownership and management through a legally binding agreement, businesses can ensure compliance with relevant laws and regulations related to succession planning and business ownership.

Overall, buy/sell arrangements are an integral part of successful succession planning, providing the necessary structure, clarity, and protection for all parties involved. Businesses that prioritize this aspect of their planning are better equipped to navigate ownership changes smoothly, safeguard business continuity, and position themselves for long-term success. Whether it's a family-owned enterprise or a corporation with multiple stakeholders, a well-crafted buy/sell agreement is a prudent investment in securing the future of the business.

FACTORS TO CONSIDER WHEN DEVELOPING A BUY/SELL ARRANGEMENT

Developing a buy/sell arrangement is a crucial aspect of business planning, especially for partnerships and closely held corporations, but it is essential to ensure that the agreement to make is well-informed and suits your interests. Here are the key factors to consider when developing a buy/sell arrangement:

- **Parties Involved:** Clearly identify all parties who will be bound by the buy/sell arrangement. This typically includes business owners or shareholders, but it can also involve key employees or other stakeholders.
- **Triggering Events:** Define the specific triggering events that will activate the buy/sell agreement, such as the death of a shareholder, disability, retirement, resignation, bankruptcy, divorce, or any other predetermined circumstances.
- **Valuation Method:** Determine the method used to determine the value of the business or the selling owner's interest. Common valuation methods include market value, book value, earnings-based multiples, or an independent appraisal.
- **Funding Mechanism**: Decide on the funding mechanism for the buyout. There are several options, including cash reserves, installment payments, sinking funds, borrowing, or insurance policies (such as life or disability insurance).
- **Insurance Considerations:** If life or disability insurance is used as a funding mechanism, carefully select the insurance policy, beneficiaries, and policy terms to ensure adequate coverage for the buyout.
- **Rights and Restrictions:** Outline the rights and restrictions related to the sale of shares. This can include first refusal rights, non-compete clauses, and restrictions on selling to external parties.
- **Payment Terms:** Define the terms of payment for the buying party. Will it be a lump-sum payment, installments over time, or a combination of both?
- **Dispute Resolution:** Include provisions for resolving potential disputes that may arise during the buyout process. Mediation or arbitration clauses can be helpful in avoiding costly litigation.

- **Updating and Reviewing the Agreement:** Specify the process for updating and reviewing the buy/sell arrangement periodically to ensure it remains relevant and aligned with the business's changing circumstances.
- **Legal and Tax Implications**: Consult with legal and tax advisors to ensure the buy/sell agreement complies with applicable laws and regulations and has the desired tax implications for all parties involved.

Developing a well-thought-out buy/sell arrangement requires careful consideration of these factors and collaboration among all parties involved. Engaging professional advisors, such as attorneys, accountants, and financial planners, can help ensure that the agreement meets the specific needs of the business and its stakeholders.

CHAPTER TEN
BUSINESS TAXES

In the complex world of business taxation, understanding the various types of taxes is essential for every business owner. Three fundamental types of business taxes that demand attention are corporate taxes, payroll taxes, and sales taxes. Delving into the specifics of each tax will enable business owners to navigate the intricate landscape of taxation with sound knowledge and adaptability.

Corporate taxes primarily apply to companies that have been incorporated as legal entities separate from their owners. This tax is levied on the corporation's profits, ensuring that a portion of the earnings is contributed towards government revenue. Corporate taxes are crucial for financing public services and infrastructure, while also ensuring fairness and an equitable distribution of the tax burden across businesses.

Payroll taxes, on the other hand, are imposed on wages paid to employees by employers. These taxes include funds allocated for Social Security and Medicare, aiding in the provision of income support and healthcare for the elderly and disabled populations. Understanding payroll taxes can prevent legal issues, such as misclassifying employees or failing to withhold the correct amount from their paychecks.

Lastly, sales taxes are imposed on the sale of goods and services at the point of purchase. This tax is typically paid by the consumer but collected and remitted by the business. It is crucial for business owners to accurately calculate and collect sales taxes to ensure compliance with the law and avoid penalties or legal consequences.

While corporate taxes, payroll taxes, and sales taxes are not an exhaustive list of business taxes, they represent the key elements that every business owner should have comprehensive knowledge about. By understanding these taxes, business owners can safeguard their businesses against unnecessary risks, promote financial stability, and foster compliance, thereby contributing positively to the broader economy.

Corporate taxes differ from other types of business taxes in a few ways:

1. Taxation entity: Corporate taxes are specifically levied on corporations, which are separate legal entities from their owners/shareholders. Other types of business taxes, such as sole proprietorship or partnership taxes, are filed and paid by the individual owners on their personal income tax returns.

2. Tax rates: Corporate taxes typically have different tax rates compared to other business structures. The rates can vary depending on the country, state, or size of the corporation. In many cases, corporate tax rates are generally higher than individual tax rates.

3. Taxable income: Corporations are taxed on their net income, which is calculated by deducting operating expenses, salaries, interest payments, and other eligible deductions from their revenue. Other business structures, like partnerships or sole proprietorships, pass their profits and losses on to the owners, who then pay taxes on their share of the income.

4. Filing requirements: Corporations need to file separate tax returns, typically known as Form 1120 or its variations, reporting the company's financial information and tax liability. Other business structures do not have separate tax filing requirements as the owners report their business income and expenses on their personal tax returns.

5. Deductions and credits: Corporations may have access to certain deductions and tax credits that are specifically designed for business entities. These deductions can include expenses like salaries, interest, research and development costs, and depreciation, among others. Some jurisdictions also provide tax credits for hiring employees, investing in research, or promoting certain industries.

6. Compliance and reporting: Corporate taxes often require more complex compliance and reporting processes, including bookkeeping, financial statements, and documentation requirements. Large corporations may also undergo audits by tax authorities to ensure compliance with tax laws.

7. Tax planning opportunities: Due to the complexity of corporate taxes, there are more opportunities for tax planning and strategies that can help minimize the overall tax liability of a corporation. This can include methods like income shifting, profit allocation, utilization of tax incentives, and other lawful strategies to optimize the tax position. However, such planning options are typically limited for other forms of business entities.

It's important to note that taxation laws vary across jurisdictions, so the specifics of corporate taxes can differ from one country to another. Consulting a tax professional or accountant is recommended for accurate and up-to-date information on corporate tax regulations.

The key differences in the calculation and collection processes for corporate taxes versus payroll taxes and sales taxes are as follows:

1. Calculation Process:
- Corporate Tax: Corporate taxes are calculated based on the taxable income of a business entity. The taxable income is determined by subtracting allowable deductions and credits from the company's total income.
- Payroll Tax: Payroll taxes are calculated based on the wages or salaries paid to employees. Both employers and employees contribute a certain percentage of the employee's earnings towards payroll taxes.
- Sales Tax: Sales taxes are calculated based on the final sale price of goods or services. The tax rate is typically a percentage of the transaction value, which can vary depending on the jurisdiction and specific products or services.

2. Collection Process:
- Corporate Tax: Corporate taxes are usually paid by companies directly to the tax authorities. The tax amount is reported and paid annually or quarterly through corporate tax returns.
- Payroll Tax: Payroll taxes are collected through a withholding system, where employers deduct the required amount from each employee's paycheck. These withheld taxes are then remitted to tax authorities on a regular basis.
- Sales Tax: Sales taxes are collected by businesses at the point of sale. The responsibility of collecting and remitting sales taxes to the tax authorities lies with the business, whether they are a retailer or a service provider. This can

be done on a monthly, quarterly, or annual basis, depending on the jurisdiction.

3. Reporting Requirements:
- Corporate Tax: Companies are required to file detailed corporate tax returns, providing information about their income, deductions, credits, and other relevant financial data. Often, extensive financial statements are also required to support the tax return.
- Payroll Tax: Employers must report and remit payroll taxes regularly, usually on a monthly or quarterly basis. They also need to provide reports to both tax authorities and employees, summarizing the amount of wages, taxes withheld, and contributions made.
- Sales Tax: Businesses are required to keep accurate records of their sales transactions, including the amount of sales tax collected. They need to report these details periodically to the tax authorities and submit the tax payments accordingly.

Overall, while corporate taxes are based on a company's income, payroll and sales taxes are connected to wages and sales, respectively. Corporate taxes are typically paid by the corporation, payroll taxes involve contributions from both employers and employees, and sales taxes are collected from consumers at the time of purchase. Additionally, reporting requirements and the frequency of payments can vary between these three types of taxes.

Corporate Taxes:

Reporting requirements: Corporations are required to file an annual tax return, known as the corporate income tax return. This return provides details of the company's income, deductions, and credits. Corporations may also be required to provide additional information, such as financial statements and supporting schedules.

Deadlines: The deadline for filing corporate tax returns typically depends on the company's fiscal year-end. In the United States, for example, the deadline is generally the 15th day of the third month following the end of the fiscal year. However, extensions may be available for corporations that require more time to file.

Remittance: Corporate taxes are typically paid through quarterly estimated tax payments. Corporations are required to estimate their tax liability for the year and make payments throughout the year to meet their tax obligations. These estimated payments are reconciled when the annual tax return is filed, and any remaining balance is remitted.

Payroll Taxes:

Reporting requirements: Employers are required to report payroll taxes on a regular basis. This includes withholding federal income tax, Social Security tax, Medicare tax, and any applicable state and local taxes. Employers must provide employees with W-2 forms detailing their wages, taxes withheld, and other relevant information.

Deadlines: Payroll taxes must be reported and remitted on a regular basis. In the United States, for example, employers generally must deposit payroll taxes either monthly or semi-weekly, depending on the size of their payroll. Employers are also required to file quarterly and annual tax returns, reporting wages, taxes withheld, and other related information.

Remittance: Payroll taxes are typically remitted to the tax authorities either monthly or semi-weekly, depending on the employer's deposit schedule. The taxes withheld from employees' wages, along with the employer's share of Social Security and Medicare taxes, are remitted to the tax authorities.

Sales Taxes:

Reporting requirements: Sales taxes are typically reported based on the specific rules of each jurisdiction. Businesses must track and report their taxable sales, including the amount of sales tax collected from customers. These records are generally required to be kept for a certain period.

Deadlines: Sales tax filing and remittance deadlines vary by jurisdiction. Some jurisdictions require monthly reporting and remittance, while others may have quarterly or annual requirements. It is important for businesses to check with the respective tax authorities to determine their specific deadlines.

Remittance: Sales tax remittance is the responsibility of the business. The collected sales tax is held in trust by the business and then remitted to the tax authorities as per the specified deadline. The remittance typically includes the total amount of sales tax collected during the reporting period.

It is important to note that reporting requirements and deadlines can vary by jurisdiction, and businesses should consult with their local tax authorities or professional tax advisors for specific guidance.

CHAPTER ELEVEN

BUSINESS DISSOLUTION

Closing a business is never an easy decision, but it is a reality that all owners or partners must face at some point in their entrepreneurial journey. Whether it is a conscious choice or the result of unforeseen circumstances, the process of closing a business requires careful planning and a systematic approach. The Small Business Administration (SBA) outlines several crucial steps that need to be undertaken to dissolve a business.

1. **Announcement:** Firstly, it is imperative to inform all partners and stakeholders about the intent to close the business. This should be done in a formal and transparent manner, ensuring that all parties are on the same page. Clear communication is vital during this stage, as it allows for open discussions and negotiations regarding the closure process.

2. **Financial Obligations:** Owners should settle any remaining financial obligations, including paying off outstanding debts, taxes, and employee wages. It is essential to fulfill these responsibilities ethically and promptly, ensuring that the business exits the market without any lingering financial burdens.

3. **Legal Obligations:** Legal obligations must be addressed. This includes cancelling business licenses, permits, and registrations, and notifying relevant authorities about the closure. Compliance with legal requirements guarantees a smooth dissolution process and protects the business owners from any potential legal repercussions.

4. **Asset and Inventory Disposal:** Owners should decide for the disposal or distribution of assets and inventory. Selling off assets or

liquidating inventory can help recoup some of the investments made in the business and minimize financial losses.

5. **Formal Dissolution:** Lastly, it is crucial to formally dissolve the business entity. This involves submitting the necessary paperwork to the relevant government agencies, such as the Secretary of State or the Internal Revenue Service. By officially dissolving the business, owners can ensure that they are no longer responsible for any future liabilities or legal obligations.

In conclusion, closing a business is a challenging task that requires careful planning and execution. Whether it is a personal decision or a result of uncontrollable circumstances, following the steps outlined by the Small Business Administration can facilitate a seamless closure process. By being transparent, fulfilling financial and legal obligations, and properly dissolving the business, owners can exit the market with integrity and pave the way for future opportunities.

REASONS FOR DISSOLUTION

There are several common reasons why business owners or partners may choose to close their business or dissolve partnerships:

i. **Financial difficulties:** Inadequate cash flow, declining revenues, or mounting debts can lead to financial distress and make it challenging to sustain the business.

ii. **Differences in goals or visions:** Partners may have diverging opinions on the future direction of the business, leading to conflicts and a decision to dissolve the partnership.

iii. **Personal or health reasons:** Personal or health issues of the business owner or partners may necessitate the closure or dissolution of the business.

iv. **Lack of profitability:** If the business is consistently unprofitable or fails to generate sufficient profits to support its operations, the owners may choose to close the business or dissolve the partnership.

v. **Retirement:** Business owners or partners reaching retirement age may opt to close the business or dissolve the partnership as part of their retirement plan.

vi. **Legal disputes or lawsuits:** Ongoing legal issues, such as lawsuits or contract disputes, can create significant financial and reputational risks for the business, leading to a decision to close or dissolve.

vii. **Market changes or disruption:** Rapidly changing market conditions, technological advancements, or industry disruptions may make it difficult for the business to stay competitive, prompting the owners to consider closure.

viii. **Disagreements or irreconcilable differences:** Partnership disputes or disagreements among owners regarding business decisions, management style, or division of responsibilities can lead to the dissolution of partnerships.

ix. **Lack of interest or burnout:** Business owners or partners may lose interest or become burnt out after years of running the business, leading to a decision to close or exit the partnership.

x. **Inadequate growth or expansion opportunities:** If the business fails to grow as expected or lacks viable opportunities for expansion, owners may decide to close or dissolve the business to pursue other ventures.

It is important to note that the reasons for closing a business or dissolving partnerships can vary significantly depending on the specific circumstances and individual motivations of the owners or partners.

A LOSS OF PASSION

When an owner or partner no longer has a passion for the business or wishes to dissolve the partnership, several steps should be taken to ensure a smooth transition and minimize potential negative impacts. These steps include:

1. **Self-reflection and communication:** The owner or partner should assess their feelings and reasons for losing passion or desiring to dissolve the partnership. Open and honest communication with the other partners or stakeholders is essential to ensure transparency and discuss potential solutions or alternatives.

2. **Legal consultation:** Consult with a business attorney or legal professional to understand the legal obligations, consequences, and options available based on the business structure and governing documents (e.g., partnership agreement, articles of incorporation).

3. **Review partnership agreement or relevant documents:** Carefully review the partnership agreement, articles of incorporation, or any other relevant documents that outline the procedures for dissolving the partnership or transferring ownership. These documents may provide guidance on how to handle such situations.

4. **Negotiate a buyout or transfer of ownership:** If the owner or partner wishes to exit but others want to continue the business, negotiation for a fair buyout or transfer of ownership should be initiated. This may involve assessing the business's value, negotiating a price, and drafting legal agreements to facilitate the transfer.

5. **Business valuation:** If necessary, engage the services of a professional business valuator to assess the value of the business accurately. This will help determine a fair buyout price and ensure both parties are satisfied with the financial aspects of the dissolution or share transfer.

6. **Consider alternative solutions:** If the owner or partner no longer wants to be involved but the other stakeholders wish to continue, explore alternatives such as finding a replacement partner, selling the business outright, or seeking external investment to buy out the exiting partner.

7. **Develop a dissolution or transition plan:** Create a detailed plan that outlines the timeline, responsibilities, and tasks involved in the dissolution or transition of the business. This plan should include considerations such as asset distribution, customer communication, financial obligations, and legal requirements.

8. **Seek professional advice:** Engaging business advisors, accountants, or consultants can provide expertise and guidance throughout the dissolution or ownership transfer process. These professionals can assist with financial matters, tax implications, and ensure compliance with regulatory requirements.

9. **Notify stakeholders and customers:** Once the plan is in place, it is important to inform all relevant stakeholders, including employees, customers, suppliers, and partners, about the planned dissolution or ownership transition. Clear communication will help manage their expectations and minimize disruption.

10. **Follow legal requirements:** Ensure compliance with any legal obligations, such as dissolution filing requirements with government agencies, notifying creditors, or settling outstanding debts.

11. **Wind down operations:** If the decision is to dissolve the business entirely, wind down operations in an orderly manner. This includes documenting financial records, fulfilling legal obligations, settling outstanding debts and liabilities, and closing accounts with relevant authorities.

Remember, it is always advisable to seek professional advice and legal assistance specific to your situation when dealing with business ownership transitions or partnership dissolutions.

When an owner or partner no longer has a passion for the business or wishes to dissolve the partnership, several steps should be taken to ensure a smooth transition and minimize potential negative impacts. These steps include:

1. Self-reflection and communication: The owner or partner should assess their feelings and reasons for losing passion or desiring to dissolve the partnership. Open and honest communication with the other partners or stakeholders is essential to ensure transparency and discuss potential solutions or alternatives.

2. Legal consultation: Consult with a business attorney or legal professional to understand the legal obligations, consequences, and options available based on the business structure and governing documents (e.g., partnership agreement, articles of incorporation).

3. Review partnership agreement or relevant documents: Carefully review the partnership agreement, articles of incorporation, or any other relevant documents that outline the procedures for dissolving the partnership or transferring ownership. These documents may provide guidance on how to handle such situations.

4. Negotiate a buyout or transfer of ownership: If the owner or partner wishes to exit but others want to continue the business, negotiation for a fair buyout or transfer of ownership should be initiated. This may involve assessing the business's value, negotiating a price, and drafting legal agreements to facilitate the transfer.

5. Business valuation: If necessary, engage the services of a professional business valuator to assess the value of the business accurately. This will help determine a fair buyout price and ensure both parties are satisfied with the financial aspects of the dissolution or share transfer.

6. Consider alternative solutions: If the owner or partner no longer wants to be involved but the other stakeholders wish to continue, explore alternatives such as finding a replacement partner, selling the business outright, or seeking external investment to buy out the exiting partner.

7. Develop a dissolution or transition plan: Create a detailed plan that outlines the timeline, responsibilities, and tasks involved in the dissolution or transition of the business. This plan should include considerations such as asset distribution, customer communication, financial obligations, and legal requirements.

8. Seek professional advice: Engaging business advisors, accountants, or consultants can provide expertise and guidance throughout the dissolution or ownership transfer process. These professionals can assist with financial matters, tax implications, and ensure compliance with regulatory requirements.

9. Notify stakeholders and customers: Once the plan is in place, it is important to inform all relevant stakeholders, including employees, customers, suppliers, and partners, about the planned dissolution or ownership transition. Clear communication will help manage their expectations and minimize disruption.

10. Follow legal requirements: Ensure compliance with any legal obligations, such as dissolution filing requirements with government agencies, notifying creditors, or settling outstanding debts.

11. Wind down operations: If the decision is to dissolve the business entirely, wind down operations in an orderly manner. This includes documenting

financial records, fulfilling legal obligations, settling outstanding debts and liabilities, and closing accounts with relevant authorities.

Remember, it is always advisable to seek professional advice and legal assistance specific to your situation when dealing with business ownership transitions or partnership dissolutions.

OWNER DEATH OR DISABILITY

The Small Business Administration (SBA) does not specifically outline procedures for dissolving a business in the event of an owner's death or disability. However, here are some general steps you can follow to ensure a smooth transition or closure of operations:

1. Establish a plan: As a business owner, it is essential to have a succession plan in place before any unforeseen event occurs. This plan should outline how the business will be transferred or closed in the event of your death or disability.

2. Identify a successor: If you intend to transfer ownership, identify a capable individual or group to take over the business. This could be a family member, key employee, or a third party willing to purchase the business.

3. Seek legal advice: Consult an attorney experienced in business succession planning to ensure compliance with applicable laws and regulations. They can help navigate any legal complexities and develop appropriate agreements or contracts to facilitate the transition.

4. Prepare necessary legal documentation: This may include a will, a power of attorney, and/or a buy-sell agreement. These documents will help determine how the business assets and responsibilities will be handled upon your death or disability.

5. Notify relevant parties: Inform key stakeholders, such as business partners, employees, customers, suppliers, or lenders, about the plan for business transfer or closure. This enables them to prepare for the transition and minimize any potential disruptions.

6. Review insurance policies: Check your insurance coverage to determine if there is any business interruption insurance or key person insurance that can financially support the transition or closure process.

7. Evaluate financial obligations: Assess any outstanding debts, loans, leases, or contracts the business has. Determine how these financial obligations will be handled or resolved during the transition or closure.

8. Liquidate or transfer assets: If closing the business, determine the best approach to liquidate assets such as inventory, equipment, or property. If transferring ownership, establish the terms for the sale or transfer of assets and update the necessary documentation.

9. Follow tax obligations: Work with an accountant to ensure proper tax filings, payments, and compliance during the transition or closure process. This includes filing final tax returns for the business and addressing any outstanding tax matters.

10. Close accounts and dissolve the business: Once all necessary steps have been completed, close business accounts, cancel business licenses and permits, notify government agencies, and dissolve the business entity officially.

While these steps provide general guidance, it is important to customize your approach based on the specific details and legal requirements of your business. Seeking professional advice and guidance is crucial to ensure compliance and a smooth transition or closure.

Book recommendation

1. THE INNOVATOR'S DILEMMA BY CLAYTON M CHRISTENSEN
2. OTHER PEOPLE'S MONEY BY JOHN KAY
3. THE DIARY OF A CEO WITH STEVEN BARTLETT (PODCAST)
4. CRYSTAL CLEAR COMMUNICATION BY GARY S GOODMAN
5. ENTERPRENEUR: WARREN BUFFETT BY DAVE O'BRIAN
6. THE POWER BROKE BY DAYMOND JOHN, DANIEL PAISNER
7. THE FINANCIAL Guidelines TO PROSPERITY, FINANCIAL SECURITY, AND WELLNESS BY FRANK BONHOMME.
8. **We are all searching for something. Love, Acceptance, Happiness's-Jesus is the answer! BY FRANK BONHOMME**

www.ingramcontent.com/pod-product-compliance
Lightning Source LLC
LaVergne TN
LVHW022050200926
848481LV00003B/849
9798223549741